WHERE IS GOD?

WHERE IS GOD?

WILLIAM JANNEN

"MAN SHALL NOT SEE ME AND LIVE"
(EXODUS 33:20)

iUniverse, Inc.
Bloomington

Where Is God?
"Man Shall Not See Me and Live" (Exodus 33:20)

iUniverse books may be ordered through booksellers or by contacting:

iUniverse
1663 Liberty Drive
Bloomington, IN 47403
www.iuniverse.com
1-800-Authors (1-800-288-4677)

Because of the dynamic nature of the Internet, any web addresses or links contained in this book may have changed since publication and may no longer be valid. The views expressed in this work are solely those of the author and do not necessarily reflect the views of the publisher, and the publisher hereby disclaims any responsibility for them.

Any people depicted in stock imagery provided by Thinkstock are models, and such images are being used for illustrative purposes only.

Certain stock imagery © Thinkstock.

ISBN: 978-1-4502-8086-0 (sc)
ISBN: 978-1-4502-8088-4 (dj)
ISBN: 978-1-4502-8087-7 (ebk)

Printed in the United States of America

iUniverse rev. date: 02/10/2011

CONTENTS

ONE

WHERE IS GOD?

Prophets, theologians, and religious writers have insisted for thousands of years that God is ineffable, unknowable, and utterly beyond anything we could imagine or experience. In short, when we talk about God, we do not know what we are talking about. People may have what they call "transcendent" or "spiritual" experiences and claim that such experiences are God, or at least put them in touch with God, but all major religions "agree that it is impossible to describe this transcendence in normal conceptual language."[1] A Roman Catholic New Testament scholar warns, for example, that we "must remember that before the mystery of God, all language must eventually fall away, and worship must fall silent to be true."[2] There is a lot to be said for silence with regard to religion. Silence would have saved us all a great deal of trouble.

---

1   Karen Armstrong, *A History of God* (New York: Ballantine Books, 1993), xxi.

2   Luke Timothy Johnson, *The Creed* (New York: Doubleday, 2004), 86.

1

But the debate goes on, and people rarely change their minds. Atheists do not become believers; believers do not become atheists. Faced with that impasse, the argument then turns not on whether there is a God or on the truth or untruth of any particular religious doctrine but on whether you personally experience a spiritual dimension that reveals God. God must come to you. It is not at all clear what it means to experience a spiritual dimension, but all religious people insist upon it; without it, you cannot find God. Those who do not experience that spiritual dimension are baffled by what religious believers try to profess.

The foregoing paragraphs seem to me to summarize the entire history of religious debate. The difficulty has always been that if the traditional tests of historical and scientific verification are abandoned—and everything turns on the individual's inward experience of the spiritual dimension—then there are no limits to what can be claimed as religious truth or revelation[3] and no agreed-upon method of verifying those claims.

Perhaps we should consider that the entire God debate is beside the point. What matters, suggests an orthodox rabbi, is trying to make life bearable by offering "redemption from the inadequacies of finitude and, mainly, from the flux of temporality."[4] Karen Armstrong, a former Roman Catholic nun and now an author who focuses on religious topics, writes that she would have been spared a great deal of suffering if her early teachers had told her "that in an important sense God was a product of the imagination, like

3   Marcus Borg, "An Appreciative Disagreement," in *Jesus & the Restoration of Israel: A Critical Assessment of N. T. Wright's Jesus and the Victory of God*, ed. Carey C. Newman (Illinois: InterVarsity Press, 1999), 232.

4   Joseph B. Soloveitchik, *The Lonely Man of Faith* (New York: Doubleday, 1965, 1992), 105.

poetry and music."[5] Elaine Pagels, a Protestant professor of religion at Princeton, wonders how being a Christian became belief in doctrine when what attracted her and, presumably, early believers was the comfort they received from a community that shared a spiritual need.[6]

All of these writers reveal a deeply felt religious sensibility, but they cannot find God! The great monotheistic traditions have all come to regard and to adhere to a set of documents as "sacred scripture," and their followers spend enormous effort—literally mountains of paper—to demonstrate that *their* scripture and not some other is God's word. Why do we have all these bizarre and wildly unbelievable tales of how God formed the world and delivered the word to particular communities? If God is otherwise remote and unknowable, then figures have to be created who can reveal and speak for God—angels, spirits, prophets, and holy men—together with stories and miracles to establish that these figures speak for God. Without them, God disappears.

How have the major monotheistic traditions dealt with a God who is never there?

---

5   Armstrong, *A History of God*, xx.
6   Elaine Pagels, *Beyond Belief* (New York: Random House, 2005), 5–6.

TWO

THE FIRST MONOTHEISTS

The ancient world was full of gods. They came and went freely. They could take human form, interact with people, enjoy sex with them, and impregnate the women. The gods were powerful and could protect people. They could be dangerous if they were angry. It was necessary to placate the gods with temples, sacrifices, and cultic practices to be safe. Many pagan religions told stories of their gods' mighty deeds and how they had made the world. Life was short, arbitrary, and inexplicable in any event. People needed the stories and the myths to make sense of it all.

Some four thousand years ago, Hebrew speaking tribes of the Near East began telling stories and legends about how their god had created the world and was the only god they could worship. The Hebrew Bible wastes no time in proclaiming that it contains the word of God. In Genesis, God talks to Abraham at length, establishing a covenant with the Israelites. After Abraham, there are no more face-to-face conversations with God. Moses hears

God's voice from Mount Sinai, where God delivers the Pentateuch in blinding smoke and flame. Moses wants to see God, but God makes it clear that "man shall not see me and live" (Exodus 33:20).[7] Thereafter, no one sees or talks with God. God speaks to humankind only through heavenly voices, angels, spirits, and, particularly, holy prophets. Every monotheistic religion since then has followed those rules and had to wrestle with the problem of whether it is really God's voice they are hearing or reading.

Eventually, the Israelites developed the doctrine that theirs was the *only* God. Not only was it true that the people of Israel—as they called themselves—could worship no other God, but there was no other God to worship. This took a while. First, their God, Yahweh, had to show he was able to protect them. Since prehistoric times, only power, prosperity, and victory in war could establish a god's divinity.

According to the Hebrew Bible, the Israelite God, Yahweh, showed himself to be a powerful warrior God by leading the enslaved Israelites out of Egypt, getting them across the Red Sea by parting it to create a pathway, and destroying the pursuing Egyptian army by letting the water come flooding back. Having successfully freed the Jews, Yahweh demanded, through Moses on Mount Sinai, that the people of Israel worship no other gods before him. If they kept that promise, or covenant, they would be his special people and enjoy his special protection. But if they broke the covenant and turned to other gods, he would destroy them mercilessly. Eventually, Yahweh came to insist there were no other gods, he was the only god, and the Israelites were his chosen people. The worship of other gods was idolatry. That is the

---

7   All biblical references are to the Revised Standard Version of 1952.

backbone myth of the Bible's Old Testament as it evolved over a period of some four thousand years.[8]

The gods of all the ancient peoples were expected to protect them from their enemies. A god that could not defeat its people's enemies would find it difficult to command their loyalty against a stronger, victorious god. There was no particular penalty for following other gods in addition to the tribal or local favorite; you never knew where you might need help. Over the centuries, however, the Israelites came to believe in a different god. Their Yahweh insisted that they worship only him, in good times and bad, and whether their God defeated their enemies or not. That was asking a lot. Moreover, a catastrophe or defeat did not necessarily mean that Yahweh had been defeated by some stronger god; Yahweh might be punishing the Israelites because they had failed to live up to their promise to be loyal and not wander off to other gods in hard times.

The Jews could be punished terribly by Yahweh, and it was not always easy to distinguish defeat by a stronger god and punishment from Yahweh. Jews puzzled over their misfortunes. If they were God's chosen people, why were they oppressed by foreign nations? Why were their tribes scattered, their kingdoms defeated and destroyed, and their people exiled and condemned to slavery?

In the course of centuries, the tales, the laments, the laws, and the traditions were committed to writing and gradually assembled with other documents. The documents in the royal archives of Israel in the north disappeared when the kingdom of Israel was defeated and destroyed by the Assyrians in 724 BCE. A second group of

---

8   Karen Armstrong, *A History of God*, 5–6, 40–41, and *passim*; Nicholas Wade, *The Faith Instinct* (New York: The Penguin Press, 2009), 149–157.

documents was held in the southern kingdom of Judah. These were further divided when Babylon defeated Judah in 587 BCE. Some continued to be held by those who did not go into exile but stayed in Jerusalem. A third and far larger group of documents was taken by those sent to Babylon and were kept there during the so-called Babylonian captivity, which lasted from 587 to 538, when the exiles were permitted to return. The documentary basis of the Hebrew Bible then is a miscellaneous collection of documents from the royal archives of Judah, hastily assembled for transport to Babylon with the exiles, and returned to Jerusalem at the end of the exile. There, this collection was presumably put together with the documents that had remained in Jerusalem.

The various documents with their stories and narratives were slowly edited, put in order, and extensively rewritten after the return from exile in 538 BCE. This work was largely done by scribes who, in addition to being subject to Babylonian cultural influences, had numerous versions of traditional stories from which to work. We are not talking about a single book, as we have today, but a collection of scrolls, which might hold a book or two of the Hebrew scriptures and official royal papers. No single scroll would have been large enough to hold the entire Bible. Jack Miles, in trying to write a coherent story of the God of Israel from the books of the Hebrew Bible, concluded that "the most coherent way to imagine the Lord God of Israel is as the inclusion of the content of several ancient divine personalities in a single character." The literary result, since this God is a fusion of different gods from different times and cultures, is "a character with a multiple personality."[9] One has only to read the Hebrew Bible as we have it in the Old Testament to see that Miles is right.

---

9   Jack Miles, *God: A Biography*, 72.

The early stories of the Hebrew Bible record, among other things, the creation of the world, the flood, the Jewish enslavement in Egypt, the exodus from Egypt, the forty years the Hebrews spent wandering in the desert looking for the Promised Land while being fed by manna from heaven, God's giving of the law to Moses on Mount Sinai, and God's covenant with the Israelites, whom Moses had led to freedom. Moses dies at the borders of the Promised Land, and it is Joshua, following the instructions of "the Lord," who leads the Jews in a savage, genocidal city-by-city conquest of the promised land of Canaan[10] where "they utterly destroyed all in the city, both men and women, young and old, oxen, sheep, and asses, with the edge of the sword" (Joshua 6:2–21). After the Israelite conquest of Jerusalem, the Hebrew Bible records the decline and fall of the kingdoms of Israel and Judah and the lamentations and warnings of the Jewish prophets. All of that happened, if it happened at all, sometime in the thirteenth century BCE, and God's covenant with Abraham, if there was an Abraham, had to have been even earlier.

Most biblical scholars regard the Old Testament stories as pious fictions. First, the Torah, or "the Law" or "the Pentateuch" or "the Five Books of Moses"—all varying labels for the same scripture—could not have been delivered to Moses on Mount Sinai as a single document engraved on two tables of stone (Exodus 31:18). The Torah reflects individual sources by several authors covering centuries of tradition both before and after the Babylonian exile of 587 BCE. They were clearly edited together or "redacted" at some point.[11]

As for the conquest of the promised land of Canaan described in Joshua, decades of archeological excavation have failed to uncover

---

10   Miles, *God: A Biography*, 154.
11   Marc Zvi Brettler, *How to Read the Jewish Bible* (New York: Oxford University Press, 2007), 35.

any signs of an Israelite invasion of that land. If the story of the Israelite conquest of Canaan were true, one would expect to find evidence of the destruction of the major Canaanite cities datable to the time of the period described. Marc Zvi Brettler and most scholars have concluded that the claim to the complete conquest of Canaan by Israel "is false." The truth is simpler: "Many Israelites originated as Canaanites." The archeological record for an extended presence of Israelites in Egypt is equally barren.[12]

It is worth remembering, with regard to any biblical account of events, that the authors writing thousands of years ago were primarily interested in the message, not the accurate depiction of the past. From a modern historical perspective, "it is improper to speak of Abraham, Jacob, or Rachel as real figures, or as early Israelites or Jews."[13] The Old Testament can be fundamentally misunderstood "if it is uncritically viewed as a primary source." It is a historically conditioned collection of traditional tales, laws, political arguments, religious arguments, diplomatic papers, etc., that were gradually accumulated and revised over millennia. "It was not created in order to provide doctrinal tenets for the dogmatists."[14] It is revered because it has come to preserve the traditional stories of Israel and of its relationship with its God.

The collapse of Israel and Judah and the Babylonian Exile of 597–538 BCE were catastrophic defeats by pagan empires and their gods. In large part, the books of the Hebrew Bible are aimed at explaining and rectifying these catastrophes so that the Israelites would not abandon

---

12   Ibid., 96.
13   Ibid., 22–23.
14   Christoph Levin, Margaret Kohl, trans., *The Old Testament: A Brief Introduction* (Princeton and Oxford: Princeton University Press, 2005), 29, 175.

Yahweh.[15] According to Christoph Levin, "the fiction developed" that Judaism had been constituted in prehistoric times, on Mount Sinai, when God delivered the law to Moses. The catastrophes suffered by Israel and Judah did not constitute the defeat of Yahweh by pagan gods, but was Yahweh's punishment of the Jews for being disobedient to his law and following other gods. That is the central message of the Hebrew Bible and is endlessly reiterated by the biblical prophets. "In the Old Testament a religious community has 'recalled' its past in the form of divine history in order to win back its future."[16]

It should come as no surprise, therefore, that the Hebrew Bible is as much a political tract as it is a theological document. Its purpose was to preserve a tradition that the Israelites were people of the one God who had created the world for a purpose and who would care for it and intervene in it until that purpose was achieved.[17] For many Jews, this meant that God would deliver them from their oppression and bring them to the Promised Land, so long as they remained loyal to their belief in Yahweh and obeyed his law. The stories of the Hebrew Bible were never intended to be "history" or "science" in the modern sense. The oral tradition of Jewish enslavement in Egypt, the exodus led by Moses, and the covenant with God made through Moses on Mount Sinai may date from the thirteenth century BCE, but the biblical accounts of these events were not written down until about the eighth century BCE.[18] The core traditions were probably brought together in the Torah sometime during the Babylonian exile of 597–538 BCE and later.[19]

15   Levin, *The Old Testament*, 22–23; Miles, *God: A Biography*, 178–192.
16   Levin, *The Old Testament*, 23–24; Wade, *The Faith Instinct*, 155.
17   Martin Goodman, *Rome and Jerusalem: The Clash of Ancient Civilizations* (New York: Knopf, 2007), 251, 255.
18   Armstrong, *A History of God*, 12.
19   Levin, *The Old Testament*, 2, 31.

What we have in "scripture" are tales of men who claim to have heard God's word and reported what he said, like Moses and the prophets; tales of men who said that they had heard God and did what he told them, like Noah and Abraham; and tales of God acting just like the pagan gods and playing games with mortals, like Job or Abraham and his beloved son. It has been known for over a century that the Hebrew Bible stories were mythical tales that the Israelites and their forebears told themselves to try to explain their place in the world.[20] To insist that the Bible is—literally, in every word—the inerrant word of God is to ignore over three hundred years of biblical scholarship and most of modern science.

If the Bible story is going to be treated as a sacred historical record because it is the inspired word of God, then we have to face the fact that we do not have the original text of any book in the Bible. Not a single original Bible text exists today—not even early copies of the original texts. Since we are dealing with the evolution of an oral culture, there probably never was an "authentic" original text, but a series of stories from which to draw. There were centuries of controversy over what was and what was not "scripture"; even in the early centuries CE, rabbinical scholars and Christian divines were battling over which documents should be regarded as authoritative within their religious traditions. The battle continues today.[21]

The oldest available manuscript of part of the Hebrew Bible—a codex of the prophets—is dated 867 CE, and the oldest manuscript of the entire Old Testament in Hebrew that still exists is dated

---

20   Brettler, *How to Read the Jewish Bible*, 21, 22, 23, 38.
21   Bart D. Ehrman, *Lost Christianities: The Battles for Scripture and the Faiths We Never Knew* (New York: Oxford University Press, 2003); Elaine Pagels, *Beyond Belief: The Secret Gospel of Thomas* (New York: Random House, 2005); Id., *The Gnostic Gospels* (New York: Random House, 1979, 1989).

1008 CE.[22] After so many centuries of copying, editing, and translating, few scholars believe that the biblical texts now accepted as authoritative are identical with the original documents or the tales they recorded. We no longer have access to any original autograph copy or even early copies of the originals. We therefore have no way of knowing what any original biblical document said. If the assumption is that the closer you get to the original text, the closer you get to the word of God as it was spoken to the prophets and the apostles, then you have to admit that the word of God is inaccessible. If that is true, then you have to ask yourself on what basis the texts are "sacred." Karen Armstrong has correctly noted that the early texts of the Bible "became holy only when approached in a ritual context that set them apart from ordinary life and secular modes of thought." She also adds that the Bible "proved" that it was holy "because people continually discovered fresh ways to interpret it and found that this difficult, ancient set of documents cast light on situations that their authors would never have imagined."[23]

Biblical authors were both interpreting and creating tradition, and texts often circulated in a variety of forms both in ancient times and throughout the Second Temple period of Judaism.[24] Revelation did not mean that every word of scripture had to be accepted. Revelation came from the constant study, interpretation, and discussion of the texts. Between 135 and 160 CE, these discussions evolved into the Mishnah, an anthology of oral teachings and discussion.[25] Well into the Christian era, copiers

---

22   Levin, *The Old Testament: A Brief Introduction*, 5.
23   Karen Armstrong, *The Bible: A Biography* (New York: Atlantic Monthly Press, 2007), 4–5.
24   Brettler, *How to Read the Jewish Bible* (2005, 2007), 22.
25   Karen Armstrong, *The Case for God* (New York: Alfred Knopf, 2009), 90–91.

of ancient manuscripts had no sense that they had to copy the manuscript exactly as it was written, so long as they captured the sense of it or could make it fit into their traditions or whatever larger project they were about. We will never know the precise words of the message from God that Moses is said to have brought down the mountain to the Jews. For those who base their religion on the inspired and inerrant word of God as recorded in the Bible, the question has to be: how do we distinguish the word of God from the word of an all-too-human author or copier or interpreter?

Debate about what should be regarded as authentic scripture has been going on for thousands of years. Even when documents were accepted as authentic scripture, the mountain of rabbinical interpretation that grew around them could be wildly divergent and contradictory. To an outsider, the Jewish religion seems like nothing so much as an endless debate over these mountains of interpretive documents. Nonetheless, the cultural and religious power of the religious documents produced by this tiny Near Eastern religion is truly stunning. Jewish scholars who reject the status of the Hebrew Bible as a historical account or revelation of the word of God still revere it as central to their religious practice, even though they are clear that the Hebrew Bible is a human, rather than a divine, work. For Marc Brettler, "It stands at the core of who I am as a person and as a Jew."[26] Christoph Levin presents the Old Testament as a collection of secular documents that still has power. Debate and interpretation should never end, for its message "announces nothing less than the new heaven and the new earth."[27] Kugel does not want to see the Hebrew Bible stripped of centuries of interpretation.

---

26   Marc Zvi Brettler, *How to Read the Jewish Bible* (Oxford, New York: Oxford University Press, 2007), 279.

27   Christoph Levin, *The Old Testament* (Princeton and Oxford, 2005), 1, 174, 176.

However human, the interpretations *are* the Bible. What matters is not that the Hebrew Bible is the inerrant word of some unknowable God; what matters is that it is sacred to a community that practices the centuries-old communal traditions of reading Torah, of schule, synagogue, Sabbath, and holidays. These scholars are Jews, and they intend to remain Jews. They do not want Jewish life and tradition to be dismantled just because they can no longer believe that Bible stories recount historical events.

Christoph Levin treats the Old Testament as a typical, ancient Middle Eastern document. He is completely secular in his presentation. "Israel, as the single, unified people of God, has never been more than a political and religious idea born in the late period." The Yahwist's history has not "unjustly" been viewed as the "Israelite national epic."[28] The stories the Old Testament tells reflect the political and religious conditions of the time in which they were written with all the polemics of ancient religious and political controversy. For Levin and others, the Israelite conquest of Canaan and its cities is pure fiction. The Torah command that "You shall have no other Gods before me" had its origins in the beginning of the postexilic period, when it appeared that Yahweh's appeal and power were being challenged by the gods of the conquering nations. "Right down to the present day, the Bible has been misused for the purposes of self-defense, and to underpin religious and even political claims, as if it came down from heaven. But the Bible is not an absolute book; it is a historical one."[29] The Hebrew Bible may be only a man-made collection of Israelite traditions, but for Levin, it is still the voice of "God's enduring promise."[30]

---

28 Levin, *The Old Testament*, 69, 129.
29 Ibid., 86, 175.
30 Ibid., 176.

Marc Zvi Brettler is equally reverent. For him, the biblical books are "holy writing." That does not quite mean what the layman ordinarily understands by "holy writing." Brettler writes, "The Bible's authority and sanctity come from the community that has canonized it, and this process, rather than any particular concept of God, revelation or inspiration, has turned this group of books into my significant religious text."[31]

He emphasizes that he regards the Bible as a collection of stories and rules that evolved among the peoples of the ancient Near East. Genesis is a myth; the Exodus did not happen; Joshua did not fight the battle of Jericho and make the walls come tumbling down. Much of the matter in the Bible's historical texts is not historical. Not everything found in the work of Amos (or Isaiah, or Jeremiah, or Ezekiel) was written by Amos (or Isaiah, or Jeremiah, or Ezekiel). The psalms were not composed by David. The Song of Songs is a secular work, and much of the rest of the Bible is also, for it was influenced by secular ideology as much as by religion. But, Brettler insists, "I am, in fact, an observant Jew. I take the Bible quite seriously in my personal life.... It stands at the core of who I am as a person, and as a Jew." Brettler goes on: "In a nutshell, here is my view of the Bible as a Jew: *The Bible is a sourcebook that I—within my community—make into a textbook. I do so by selecting, revaluing, and interpreting the texts that I call sacred.*"[32] The biblical stories represent almost three thousand years of Jewish tradition, and Brettler sees no reason to dismiss them just because they are stories.

James L. Kugel's *The Bible As It Was*, opens a huge chasm between the Hebrew Bible as we now have it and any putative ancient word

---

31   Brettler, *How to Read the Jewish Bible*, viii.
32   Ibid., 279, 280, italics in the original.

of God. Kugel offers a history of Jewish interpretation of the texts of the Hebrew Bible. He makes it clear that biblical interpretation was not something that began *after* the books of the Hebrew Bible were written; interpretation and interpretive discussion were there from the beginning as the documents were assembled and the books were composed, edited, copied, translated, and debated.

The interpreters of the Hebrew Bible worked with four assumptions; they do so still, as, indeed, did their early Christian successors who were, after all, Jews themselves.[33]

1. The first assumption was that the Bible is a fundamentally cryptic document. It does not always mean what it seems to say, and the true, underlying meaning, has to be meticulously searched out. It may really be saying Y when it appears to say X. That assumption, needless to say, gave biblical interpreters considerable leeway.

2. Scripture constitutes one great book of instruction, a guide by which to interpret current affairs. Biblical figures such as Enoch, Abraham, Jacob, and Moses represent guides for other human beings. Everything was held to apply to present-day life. For Paul, for example, as for all ancient interpreters, the Bible was not *essentially* a record of things that happened or were spoken. These things may have happened, but they are in the Bible not to record but to instruct. Again, that assumption gave the interpreter great freedom in transmitting the text as a guide to life.

3. The third assumption was that the Bible was harmonious in all its parts. There were no mistakes or inconsistencies.

---

33   James L. Kugel, *The Bible as It Was* (Cambridge, MA: The Belknap Press of Harvard University Press, 1997), 18 ff.

Interpreters therefore had to discover the underlying harmony and eliminate contradictions and mistakes. Every detail was important; everything was intended to teach something. Nothing was irrelevant. It was the interpreter's task to see that this was so. Scripture was perfect.

4. The assumption that scripture was divinely inspired was addressed rather late in the history of biblical interpretation.[34] It seems reasonable to suppose that the relative absence of that discussion meant that most writers took it for granted that they were dealing with the word of God.

These four assumptions gave interpreters of scripture great leeway to make the texts conform to their views. Moreover, Hebrew scripture was written only with consonants. Contemporaries, knowing the context, might make sense of the text, but those reading the text centuries later would have great difficulty understanding it. To make matters worse, biblical texts were written without capital letters, periods, commas, or any kind of punctuation. By the time the Babylonian captivity was over and many Jews had come back to Judah, the old texts required scribes who were specialists to make sense of them for their contemporaries. The scribes exercised great freedom in their interpretations. "Carried to an extreme, the freedom of interpreters to read a single word in different ways or to break up a block of text into various syntactic combinations could at times allow them to make a text out to be saying exactly the opposite of its apparent meaning."[35] This was, of course, the extreme, but it indicates the problems scholars have in recovering the original texts.

---

34 Ibid., 23.
35 Ibid., 5.

Ancient interpretive traditions, in short, changed utterly the meaning of the Bible.[36] Indeed, according to Kugel, these interpretations essentially became the Bible as, over the centuries, authoritative interpretations came to be treated as scripture and were themselves interpreted.[37]

Nevertheless, Kugel is upset by modern methods of biblical criticism that peel away the layers of interpretation to get at the "real Bible … waiting to be discovered underneath the accumulated misconceptions of centuries." The difficulty, according to Kugel, is that the modern critical approach fails to take into account "the crucial role played by ancient interpreters in the very emergence of the Bible." Biblical study, he complains, has changed from learning from scripture to research on the Bible's origins and manner of composition. Bible study became "pre-Bible study," breaking things down to their original putative components. Modern scholars thought they could find the "real Bible" behind centuries and layers of interpretation. Instead, they were "returning the biblical texts to the state they were in before there was a Bible, which is to say, turning the unitary, seamless, Word of God into the contradictory, seamy, words of different men and schools and periods."[38] Kugel seems to be arguing that while he reveres the work of biblical interpreters, he really does not want to know about the documents from which they worked.

Still, Kugel sympathizes with the motives that led to all this: "Was it not in the ear of Moses, Isaiah, or Jeremiah that the divine word had been whispered?"[39] They were the true prophets—not

---

36   Ibid., 49.
37   Ibid., 550.
38   Ibid., 558.
39   Ibid., 559.

the commentators, re-tellers, or interpreters. But, "the activity of ancient biblical interpreters was a—perhaps *the*—striking instance of a kind of second authorship. It was *their* Bible, and not a ragtag collection of ancient Near Eastern texts, that was canonized in the closing centuries of the Second Temple period, and their Bible is, to an extent with which all who love God's word must reckon, ours today."[40] Kugel's position is much like the conservative Christian reaction to the search for the historical Jesus. The conservative Christian wants the Christ of faith as depicted in the New Testament, and in Christian art, hymns, and liturgy, not scholarly speculations on what a first-century Palestinian Jew may or may not have said and done.

This is a common attitude among religious people who cannot bring themselves to abandon the religious tradition in which they were raised. For most Jews, being heir to an ancient Jewish tradition and taking part in its practices makes one a Jew. Doubts about the divine origins of the Old Testament do not change that. There is a great deal of ambiguity and tension in such a position, and Orthodox Jews will not accept it.

For example, Rabbi Joseph B. Soloveitchik, who adheres to the Orthodox Jewish religious tradition, cannot follow a path that seems to abandon a providential creator God and does not leave the "sacredness and integrity" of the Hebrew Bible intact. Rabbi Soloveitchik is a man of faith for whom "to be means to believe." Orthodox, learned and devout, he cannot help "living by a doctrine which has no technical potential, by a law which cannot be tested in the laboratory." He is "steadfast in his loyalty to an eschatological

---

40   The last few paragraphs attempt to summarize the argument in Kugel, *The Bible as It Was*, 557–560.

vision whose fulfillment cannot be predicted with any degree of probability." He is troubled and lonely because he cannot speak his faith in "a functional, utilitarian society which is *saeculum-oriented*[41] and whose practical reasons of the mind have long ago supplanted the sensitive reasons of the heart."[42] He is lonely not because he is alone, but because, in his own words, "At times I feel rejected and thrust away by everybody, not excluding my most intimate friends,"[43] apparently because they do not share his deep, orthodox faith commitment. The rabbi is troubled because he lives in a world that believes the stories upon which he has based his faith are unbelievable and to which his faith in those stories is incomprehensible. He sees no remedy to this situation and does not think one is possible. To find relief, he writes a book: "A tormented soul finds peace in confessing."[44]

The rabbi lays out his position at the very outset.

I have never been seriously troubled by the Biblical doctrine of creation vis-à-vis the scientific story of evolution at both the cosmic and the organic levels, nor have I been perturbed by the confrontation of the mechanistic interpretation of the human mind with the Biblical spiritual concept of man. I have not been perplexed by the impossibility of fitting the mystery of revelation into the framework of historical empiricism. Moreover, I have not even been troubled by the theories of Biblical criticism which contradict the very

---

41   Soloveitchik seems to mean "focused on everyday life." See Charlton T. Lewis and Charles Short, *A Latin Dictionary* (Oxford: Clarendon Press, 1879, 1966), 1613, column 3.
42   Joseph B. Soloveitchik, *The Lonely Man of Faith* (New York: Doubleday, 1965, U.S. ed., 1992), 6–7.
43   Ibid., 3.
44   Ibid., 2, 5.

foundations upon which the sanctity and integrity of the Scriptures rest.[45]

So, science is out, historical empiricism is out, and biblical criticism is out. Rabbi Soloveitchik is not going to abandon centuries of poring over sacred scripture, nor will he allow the sacredness of scripture to depend on the practices of observant but less orthodox Jewish communities, as Brettler, Kugel, and Levin do. This faith commitment has a price: existential loneliness, despair, and an inability to make his spiritual dilemma understood in the modern world.

As rabbis have done for thousands of years, Rabbi Soloveitchik offers an interpretation of the true meaning of Genesis, which will explain away the plain fact that it contains two separate creation stories. He rejects "the theory suggested by Bible critics attributing these two accounts to two different traditions and sources" because "we unreservedly accept the unity and integrity of the Scriptures and their divine character."[46] The answer does not lie in an "alleged dual tradition but in dual man, not in an imaginary contradiction between two versions, but in a real contradiction in the nature of man."[47] This is sheer speculation, based solely on the fact that the rabbi cannot accept that there are two separate traditions underlying the two Genesis creation stories.

In Genesis I, God creates man in his own image and gives him dominion over all the earth. In Genesis II, God formed man from the dust of the earth, breathed life into his nostrils, and placed him in the Garden of Eden to take care of it. God has blessed Adam I with "the human mind, capable of confronting the outside world

---

45   Ibid., 6–7.
46   Ibid., 9–10.
47   Ibid., 9–11.

and inquiring into its complex workings."[48] In directing Adam I to subdue nature, God directed Adam's attention to the functional and practical aspects of his intellect. Adam I asks only how the cosmos functions; he is not interested in why the cosmos functions at all. He does not want to know its essence, just how it works.[49] He can be religious and go to church, but religion is just a useful part of his life. It is not a real faith commitment. Adam I is driven by a desire to harness and dominate elemental natural forces so that he can put them at his disposal. God created him that way.

Adam II, on the other hand, wants to confront the great mystery of *being*. He does not ask a single functional question. He wonders why the world in its totality came into existence. He asks what there is beyond the material world that haunts him so. It is this double nature of man—a duality that God created—that is reflected in the two creation stories, and the rabbi's book asks whether there is a spiritual "more" beyond the material world, which we can touch and see. Adam II suffers from existential loneliness because of it. Adam I does not even know what it is.

Adam I clearly represents modern man and the material world; Adam II "knows" there is a spiritual world beyond the world of Adam I, and Adam II is troubled because Adam I seems not to need that world. Adam II suffers torments of loneliness in his life of the spirit, a life that "is his and only his, and it would make no sense if disclosed to others."[50] The rabbi is right: if you do not "experience" God, you will not find him. The dilemma confronting the modern man of faith is "insoluble." Why is it insoluble? Because, while he feels God and the spirit, he cannot convincingly demonstrate their

---

48   Ibid., 12.
49   Ibid., 12–13.
50   Ibid., 67.

existence. God haunts him and then disappears at the very instant he turns to look for him. For Soloveitchik, as for other theologians, God is unknowable and "abides in the recesses of transcendental solitude." The "very moment man turns his face to God, he finds Him remote, unapproachable, enveloped in transcendence and mystery."[51]

The irony is that, Adam I, as described by the rabbi, seems perfectly content in his material, technological world. What the rabbi seems to fear is that the world of Adam I may forget the spiritual dimension of existence. He may not find redemption. As the rabbi presents the problem, there is really nothing much Adam I can do and not much reason to try. The rabbi is convinced there is a world of the spirit underlying the material world, but it can be reached only by a real faith commitment. Such faith "is born of the intrusion of eternity upon temporality." "Faith is experienced not as a product of some emergent evolutionary process ... but as something which has been given to man when the latter was overpowered by God." The prime goal of faith "is redemption from the inadequacies of finitude and, mainly, from the flux of temporality."[52] Man seems to be wholly passive in this process. God has to do something. He has to overpower man so he can be given faith. "When God joins the community of man the miracle of revelation takes place."[53]

Rabbi Soloveitchik's commentary on the two Genesis creation stories is essentially an essay on the nature of man. It has little or nothing to do with Genesis and could have been written without it. Like virtually every attempt to probe the spiritual world that is supposed to lie beyond the material world, it is hopelessly obscure. Does he really want the Hebrew Bible stories to be regarded as sacred

---

51   Ibid., 48, 112.
52   Ibid., 105.
53   Ibid., 53, 110.

and true? Does he want to find the God that wipes out all living creatures in a flood? The God that brings plague and death to the Egyptians and turns their rivers into blood for the sake of a tribe of Middle Eastern nomads? The God who lets Joshua conduct a campaign of ethnic cleansing in the land of Canaan for that same set of nomads? The God who torments Job just to show off his powers? The God who disappears whenever true believers seek him out? The God who has yet to deliver on any of his covenants with Israel? It is impossible to tell what it is that the rabbi wants, and he himself writes that the dilemma is "insoluble."

This dilemma has been with us for thousands of years. What is God? Where is God? Already in the fifties of the Common Era, Paul of Tarsus asked, "Who has known the mind of the Lord?" (Romans 11:34). Sometime in the thirteenth century CE, St. Thomas Aquinas admitted: "Hence, in the last resort all that man knows of God is to know that he does not know him."[54] More recently, the Roman Catholic theologian Luke Timothy Johnson has written: "Let us begin with the candid recognition that all properly religious language claims more than it can demonstrate, define, or even understand.... God's absolute otherness demands silence rather than description."[55] That, of course, has not silenced Rabbi Soloveitchik or Luke Timothy Johnson and has not prevented millions of words from being written and preached about God.

---

54   Quoted at Armstrong, *A History of God*, 205.
55   Johnson, *The Creed*, 53, 56, 66, 86, 214.

THREE

AFTER JESUS

Christianity solved the problem of a remote, unknowable god by bringing him down to earth in human form, as his son, Jesus. The problem is that most Christians no longer believe that story. Here is Marcus Borg, a Protestant New Testament scholar: "The notion that God's only son came to this planet to offer his life as a sacrifice for the sins of the world, and that God could not forgive us without that having happened, and that we are saved by believing this story, is simply incredible.... [T]aken literally, it is a profound obstacle to accepting the Christian message."[56]

Borg can no longer believe the Christian New Testament story as an account of historical events; nonetheless, taken "metaphorically," the New Testament story can be very powerful. Every religious tradition that I have looked at resorts to the term *metaphor* whenever

---

56   Marcus J. Borg, *Meeting Jesus Again for the First Time* (San Francisco: HarperSanFrancisco, 1996), 131.

it is pointed out that elements of the religious tradition in question are simply incredible.

Borg, for example, writes that Jesus was not literally the "son of God"; that phrase is a metaphor that points to Jesus as one whose relationship to God was so intimate and deep that he could be spoken of as the son of God.[57] But God for Borg is not "God" as we ordinarily understand him. God is not some being out there who knows and cares for us. God is the "sacred," the sense that there is more to the world than we can see and touch, and Jesus was a "spirit person," who was uniquely able to put ordinary mortals in touch with the spirit world. "Believing in Jesus does not mean believing doctrines about him. Rather, it means to give one's heart, one's self at its deepest level, to the post-Easter Jesus as the living Lord." Wholly apart from trying to make sense of all this, Borg then boldly announces that: "Candor compels me to acknowledge that experiences of the sacred do not prove the reality of God."[58] Here is another example from a geneticist: the longtime head of the Human Genome Project and a former atheist who, looking at Genesis 2, wondered whether the story of Adam and Eve could not be treated as a poetic and powerful allegory of God's plan for the entrance of the soul and moral law (that all people sense that there is a "right and wrong") into humanity.[59] You could. But if you do not believe the story, why would you bother?

In a rough and ready way, Judaism and Christianity combine to tell a single story. The Christian God of the New Testament is the God of Israel described in the Hebrew Bible, and that Bible told and retold the story that God had chosen Israel, would restore her fortunes,

---

57   Ibid., 109 and *passim*.
58   Ibid., 14, 38, 131, 137.
59   Francis S. Collins, *The Language of God* (New York: Free Press, 2006), 207.

and through Israel would bring the whole of creation to its intended fulfillment.[60] Christians interpret that "fulfillment" as the coming of Jesus. That is why Christians have added the New Testament stories concerning the ministry of Jesus to the documents of the Hebrew Bible to make what is now, for Christians, the Bible.

Both the Jewish and the Christian traditions agree that something went wrong after the creation: humankind was disobedient and prevented God from creating the kingdom of the righteous. In the Jewish tradition, the prophets warned over and over that the Israelite people must return to Yahweh, Israel's God, and live by the Torah, or face catastrophe. In the Christian tradition, human reform was never going to be enough. The human rebellion against the creator God "reflects a cosmic dislocation between the creator and the creation, and the world is consequently out of tune with its created intention."[61] This dislocation was so vast, so deep-seated, that God could only remedy it by doing the job himself. After millennia of inscrutable invisibility, God finally revealed himself by coming to earth and incarnating himself as a human being: Jesus. Jesus then delivers God's message to a fallen world so that it may be saved.

Jesus was a Jew. According to the Hebrew Bible, the Hebrew God, Yahweh, had chosen the Israelites to be his people. Yahweh would protect them and guide them. They would become a great nation, the light of the world. Other nations would stand in awe of Israel and its great God, Yahweh. That, over the centuries and through countless variations, was Israel's story. After the Babylonian conquest of 587 BCE, and certainly by the first century CE, that story was in shambles. Contrary to divine promises, the Davidic

---

60   N. T. Wright, *The New Testament and the People of God* (Minneapolis: Fortress Press, 1992), 77–78.
61   Ibid., 133.

royal line had come to an inglorious end. The Babylonians had destroyed Solomon's Temple. Many Jews had been led into exile by the Babylonians. Even after they were allowed to return to Jerusalem and had rebuilt what became the Second Temple, the Israelites lived under the domination of one great power after another. In Jesus's time, from roughly 4 BCE to 30 CE, it was the Romans.

The cumulative effect of these events brought about tumultuous religious diversity and social unrest within the Jewish homeland. Yahweh had delivered them from Egypt and from Babylon and brought them to the chosen land. Why were God's chosen people still ruled by pagans? What could be done? By the time Jesus appeared on the scene, he and his few followers were just one of a multitude of fiercely competing sects claiming to answer such questions and fighting bitterly over matters of Jewish observance and piety.[62]

As Geza Vermes has long reminded us, these were all Jews. Jesus believed that Jewish scripture contained the revealed word of God and that the commandments of Moses should be followed and seems to have had little or no intention of founding a new religion.[63] What we now know as Christianity did not exist until at least two generations after the death of Jesus.[64] John Dominic Crossan insists that it is hopelessly wrong to think of Christianity as a religion quite apart from Judaism in the first century. "I could speak of the kingdom-of-God movement, the Jesus movement, or the Christ movement," but they were all, including Christianity, a sect within Judaism. It was

---

62   Armstrong, *The Bible*, 55; Michael White, *From Jesus to Christianity* (San Francisco: HarperSanFrancisco, 2004), 117; Nicholas Wade, *The Faith Instinct* (New York: The Penguin Press, 2009), 158.

63   Wade, *The Faith Instinct*, 163; E. P. Sanders, *The Historical Figure of Jesus* (New York: Penguin Putnam Inc., 1993), 224; Geza Vermes, *Jesus, the Jew* (Great Britain: Fortress Press Ed., 1973, 1981).

64   White, *From Jesus to Christianity*, 13.

only decades after the death of Jesus, when the Jesus followers began to insist that Jesus was God incarnate, the true son of God, that the split between what we now know as Christians and Jews became irrevocable. The Hebrew religion was monotheistic. There was only one God, and that was Yahweh. How could Jesus be God? Crossan is not even prepared to say that Christianity eventually broke away from Judaism. Given the religious turmoil of early first-century Palestine, he believes it is more accurate to say that out of the matrix of biblical Judaism and the maelstrom of late Second-Temple Judaism and the sects, two great traditions eventually emerged: early Christianity and rabbinic Judaism—"both children of the same mother."[65]

The Jesus movement and the other competing sects appropriated the language of the Hebrew Bible prophets and claimed that God was working through them to inaugurate his long-awaited kingdom. If Israel would follow them, repent, and obey the gospel, God would restore the kingdom of Israel.[66]

Talk about "restoring Israel" was a touchy subject for the Romans. The constant hostility and recurring riots of the Jews was a particular irritation. Jews often claimed that the king of a renewed Israel would be installed by God. But the Romans had their own imperial cult that claimed that their emperors were gods. During the Passover holiday, thousands of Jews poured into Jerusalem to celebrate and worship. According to the New Testament, Jesus and his followers were among them. It is more than likely that in

---

65   John Dominic Crossan, *The Birth of Christianity* (San Francisco: Harper Collins, 1998), xxxiii; Armstrong, *The Bible*, 55–57.

66   Wade, *The Faith Instinct*, 163–164; Armstrong, *The Bible*, 55; White, *From Jesus to Christianity*, 13–35; N. T. Wright, *The New Testament and the People of God*, 338, 157–162, 216–218; Ibid., *Jesus and the Victory of God* (Minneapolis: Fortress Press, 1996), 197, 201, 334, 390, 415, 438, 473.

that heated atmosphere, someone pressed too hard on the theme of restoring the kingdom of Israel and its true king. To the Romans, that smacked of treason. It is very likely that they picked up one or more of the Jewish "prophets" surging through the streets. According to the synoptic gospels, one of them was Jesus, and those closest to Jesus fled. Jesus was then tortured and executed. There was probably not much discussion about it. This was just another Galilean peasant, and the Romans had been executing them by the thousands.[67] According to the synoptic gospels, two other men were crucified along with Jesus.

It is not clear why the Romans picked up Jesus. His ministry had not been particularly successful, and it had been around only one or two years.[68] He did not have many followers. It is hard to see how he could pose a serious political threat to the Romans. But, according to the gospels, he came to their attention and was captured, tortured, and hideously executed by crucifixion. Crucifixion was a horrible and disgraceful death, and it was Roman practice to leave the corpses hanging as a deterrent. When birds, dogs, and wild beasts had stripped the bones clean, they were tossed into an ossuary.[69]

According to the New Testament gospels, this did not happen to Jesus. Instead, a wealthy follower bribed the Romans to allow him to take the body down, put it in a newly cut burial cave, and close the cave with a heavy stone. Three days later, Mary Magdelane and Mary, the mother of Jesus, came to find the stone at the entrance rolled away, the grave empty, and a young man in bright, white clothes who told them Jesus was risen. He instructed them to tell the disciples that

67   John Dominic Crossan, *Jesus: A Revolutionary Biography* (San Francisco: HarperSanFrancisco, 1994), 152.

68   White, *From Jesus to Christianity*, 103–104.

69   Crossan, *Jesus: A Revolutionary Biography*, 123–127.

Jesus was going to Galilee to meet them. But, according to the gospel of Mark, the women were too frightened; they ran away and told no one. The gospel of Mark ends there, but the gospels of Matthew, Luke, and John go on to describe a risen Jesus eating meals and having conversations with his followers for another forty days. Then he disappears forever. That is all the gospels give us. The two women and one or two evangelists are described as seeing an empty grave, and then there are a series of appearance stories where followers of Jesus meet a man whom they believe to be Jesus.

The gospel resurrection stories and Paul's letters on the resurrection are the sole basis for the Christian religion. Without the resurrection, Jesus would have been regarded as just another in a long line of would-be but failed messiahs.[70] "If the Jesus story had ended with his crucifixion, there probably would not have been a Christian religion today."[71] N. T. Wright, the Anglican bishop of Durham, makes this point repeatedly in his massive three-volume work on Jesus and Christianity. That several people saw the empty tomb is the necessary condition for the rise of the Christian faith. Without the resurrection, any claim to being the Messiah would have been undone by the shameful death at the hands of the Roman authorities.[72] Without the resurrection, Jesus's followers would have faded back into the Jewish world of their time, returning to the Second Temple, or dispersed among the many sects making virtually the same claims as Jesus. Paul's letter to his church in Corinth, written some thirty years after the death of Jesus, makes this perfectly clear: "If Christ be not risen, then is our preaching vain, and your faith

---

70   Wright, *Jesus and the Victory of God*, 544.

71   Jim Rigas, *Christianity without Fairy Tales* (Chapel Hill, NC: Professional Press, 2004), 228; Johnson, *The Creed*, 181.

72   N. T. Wright, *The Resurrection of the Son of God* (Minneapolis, 2003), 557, 695, 717.

is also vain."[73] Paul claimed only to be saying what was preached to him. Christian theologians have said this ever since: without the resurrection of Jesus, there is no Christianity.

This is clearly no ordinary story. Perhaps we should look at it a little more carefully. Paul never met Jesus and says that he is only repeating what was "preached" to him. Moreover, Paul may be speaking of a spiritual resurrection. He rejected out of hand the idea of a corpse being resurrected and seems to argue that it was a "celestial" body that God resurrected. The gospels of Mark, Matthew, Luke, and John were written two or more decades later. But by then, they were referring to a "bodily" resurrection.[74] In the original gospel of Mark, there is no mention of any appearances by Jesus after his death, but an appearance story does appear to have been added to Mark's gospel at a later date. From then on, the later gospels all include a bodily appearance by Jesus after three days of burial.

In any case, the early Christians had no choice. Even the rigidly orthodox bishop of Durham writes that: "The resurrection, however we understand it, was the only reason they came up with for supposing that Jesus stood for anything other than a dream that might have come true but didn't."[75] A resurrection from the dead was the only way that early Christians could distinguish Jesus from the multitude of Jewish sect leaders, movement leaders, self-styled prophets, and religious spokesmen, and that was the story that they told.

New Testament scholars are virtually unanimous that the gospel writers were "far more interested in the theological significance

---

73   1 Corinthians 15:13–14.
74   1 Corinthians 15:40; Wade, *The Faith Instinct*, 170–172.
75   Wright, *Jesus and the Victory of God*, 659.

carried by the story than in its historical accuracy."[76] Bart D. Ehrman points out that "each Gospel writer has an agenda ... an understanding of Jesus he wants his readers to share."[77] E. P. Sanders writes that gospel authors wrote intending for people to turn to Jesus. Karen Armstrong's book on the Bible reminds us that the New Testament "was not interested in objective history" and that the only Jesus we know is in the New Testament.[78] Since N. T. Wright and others have already pointed out that the Jesus movement simply would not have survived without the resurrection of Jesus from the dead,[79] it should come as no surprise that the tiny group of clearly disappointed Jesus followers would come up with the bodily resurrection and subsequent ascension of Jesus to heaven.

In a massive, three-volume, 1,876-page exegesis on first-century Jewish and early Christian documents, the conservative Anglican bishop of Durham insists that the bodily resurrection actually happened. It was no mere feeling of the continuing power of Jesus. In an argument of truly awesome circularity, he argues that the ancient pagans and ancient Jews never believed that the dead could be bodily brought to life. Neither antiquity nor the Hebrew Bible ever told such a story. The early Jesus followers could not have made it up out of whole cloth. Therefore, the only way to account for the early Christian belief in the resurrection is "on the hypothesis that it was true."[80] That is a truly staggering assertion.

---

76   White, *From Jesus to Christianity*, 116.

77   Ehrman, *Lost Christianities*, 170.

78   Armstrong, *The Bible*, 55.

79   Luke Timothy Johnson, "A Historiographical Response to Wright's Jesus," in *Jesus & the Restoration of Israel*, ed. Carey C. Newman (Downers Grove, IL.: InterVarsity Press, 1929), 219.

80   Wright, *The Resurrection of the Son of God*, 6.

Given that line of argument, did the early Christians believe that when Jesus died on the cross, "the tombs were opened and many bodies of the sleeping saints came back to life and came out of the tombs after his resurrection and went into the holy city, where they appeared to many" (Matt. 27:51–53)? What kind of bodies did they have? A resuscitated corpse or transformed physicality? Is there any report outside of the gospels of this mass emptying of graves? Where did they all go?

If early Jesus followers could come up with stories like that, why would it be impossible for them to invent the resurrection? The disciples had followed Jesus for over a year, leaving home and hearth, believing they were doing God's work, expecting to be kings of the twelve tribes of Israel and arguing over who would sit at Jesus's right hand and who would have more power. How could they give all that up? Weren't they men like other men? Did they not have dreams and aspirations? How could they be the duped followers of yet another failed and executed messiah? Or the disappointed followers of yet another prophet whom Israel had ignored? They were all Second-Temple Jews; how could they convince their fellow Jews that they were the true Israel who would make Israel the light of the world when the rest of Second-Temple Jewry thought the Jesus followers were dangerous idiots. It was too much. They knew that Jesus was alive and with God; they felt it.[81]

The disciples therefore insisted that their Jesus was the embodied son of Israel's creator God and marked the climax of Israel's history. He was raised from the dead by Israel's creator God to vindicate Israel and the Jesus movement and to defeat death, defeat Satan, remove evil, and bring peace and love into the world—not just to Israel, but

---

81   Johnson, *The Creed*, 181.

to the world, since Israel, God's chosen people, had now reached the climax of its history and was vindicated in the resurrection of Jesus. That, in the main, is still the Christian story.

And it worked, didn't it? Wright spends a lot of time and hundreds of pages to show that the resurrection, the empty tomb, and the appearances are not later additions to the gospel stories; the empty tomb and the resurrection go back to the earliest Christians. That, precisely, makes my point. The disciples had to tell those stories to distinguish themselves from other movements. There was immense variety in early Christian belief, and when Roman Catholic orthodoxy became orthodoxy—and imperial orthodoxy at that—alternative doctrines and movements were gradually eliminated, their books burned, and their leaders silenced.[82]

Wright regards the finding of an empty tomb and the subsequent meetings with Jesus as "historically secure." But are they? That dual foundation is based entirely on the gospel stories. Marcus Borg comments that Wright treats the synoptic gospels as recording the literal truth as to what Jesus said and did.[83] And Luke Timothy Johnson, a Roman Catholic theologian, is prepared to argue that there is, in fact, only a single "Synoptic witness" to Wright's version of the risen Jesus, which makes Wright's historical argument a good deal less secure.[84] The people who created the oral tradition on which the gospels are based believed in and spoke with angels, believed in Satan, and believed in their creator God, who had betrayed them

---

82   Ehrman, *Lost Christianities*, 2–3, *passim*.

83   Marcus J. Borg, "An Appreciative Disagreement," in *Jesus & The Resurrection of Israel*, ed. Newman, 231.

84   Johnson, "A Historiographical Response to Wright's Jesus," Ibid., 220. It should be pointed out that Roman Catholics put a great deal less weight on Gospel evidence than do Protestants.

over and over again and left them suffering in misery for millennia but would nonetheless eventually vindicate Israel, crush her enemies, and prove himself the one true God. Now, at long last, he had done so by sacrificing Jesus, his son. What kind of historical probability do such stories from pious first-century Palestinian Jews give that would rise above the historical improbability of bringing a dead man back to life? Mark, the earliest gospel writer, has an empty tomb, but no appearances by Jesus. Wright concedes that the empty tomb by itself is no evidence for anything but grave robbery. The empty tomb plus the appearances of Jesus are not enough either; there are far too many visions, apparitions, and appearances by playful gods in the ancient world to establish that Jesus had been bodily raised from the dead. But the empty tomb and meetings with a Jesus who had a solid body and was physically alive after being buried for three days, that, Wright thinks, would give us a high degree of historical probability.

But this resurrection was not, for Wright and most Christian theologians, a resuscitated corpse. It was some kind of spiritual resurrection. Paul wrote almost two thousand years ago that you had to be a fool to think that God would bring back Jesus with merely a resuscitated human body (1 Corinthians 15:36). God gave him an incorruptible celestial body, a spiritual body (1 Corinthians 15:40, 44). Wright accepts that and calls it "transformed physicality."

Marcus Borg, who is a good friend of Wright's, has wrestled mightily with this concept, but can make no sense of it. He understands that Wright rejects that the resurrection was a resurrection of Jesus's corpse, but what is "transformed physicality"? Borg is even more baffled when he hears Wright say that the risen Christ continues to exist in heaven to this day in a state of transformed physicality. How does that work? Does he occupy space and have weight? Does he eat and digest food? Maybe such a state does not require food? "I feel like a madman," writes Borg, "asking such questions."[85] He is not alone, and the same problems exist for the bodily ascension of Mary, the mother of Jesus.

Furthermore, in the gospel of Luke, written in about 85 CE, over fifty years after the crucifixion and perhaps thirty years after Paul's letter on the event, it is clear that Jesus is talking about his body as a resuscitated corpse. "Behold my hands and feet," he admonishes the disciples. He asks them to look at his wounds. He insists that he has flesh and bones (Luke 24:39–40). Whatever happened to "transformed physicality," or Paul's insistence that flesh and blood cannot enter the kingdom of heaven (1 Corinthians 15:50)? John, too, writing toward the end of the first century, has Jesus particularly point out the wounds of his crucifixion (John 20:25). What are we to make of these appearance stories? If the grave was empty, where did the body go? If Jesus could rise with his actual body, what did he do with it? How did he get around? Paul offers a list of appearances, but it does not agree at all with the appearance stories of the four gospels, which were written later. And there is no remaining record of the appearance to five hundred at once that Paul reports (1 Corinthians 15:6). Paul's letter also refers to twelve rather than eleven apostles, so it is clear he has not yet heard the Judas story.

These varying appearance accounts probably represent the competing stories of many Christian groups that arose in the first century. The emerging church eventually destroyed the records of those groups that threatened its gradually hardening orthodoxy.[86] Only someone already committed to the New Testament stories

---

85   Marcus Borg, "An Appreciative Disagreement," Ibid., 241–242.
86   I have taken much of these last few paragraphs from Rigas, *Christianity without Fairy Tales*, 228–234.

could accept the appearances and the empty grave as "historically secure." We have to face the unfortunate fact that a mentality that can accept the physical resurrection of the dead is utterly different from ours. The resurrection story is there only to authenticate the claim that Jesus was the son of God, if not God himself. What else could Paul and the gospel writers say to make Jesus the Messiah?

There is another problem. Who, exactly, did the Romans crucify? The Jesus that Christians now worship as God? Or just another leader of a Jewish sect seeking the restoration of Israel? White lists almost three pages of zealots and extremists active at this time. Wright points out that there were a number of Jewish leadership "prophets" much like Jesus. He belonged thoroughly to the Jewish first-century world and was "neither the first nor the last" to make the claim that he was restoring Israel. "Where," asks White, "does Jesus fit in all this? How many messiahs should we expect to find?"[87]

This is a serious problem. Whose words and deeds are reported in the gospels we now have? The Jesus now worshipped by Christians or some other movement leader? Who was crucified? The disciples could not know. They ran away when Jesus was crucified. Paul certainly does not know; he never met Jesus. The gospels report two other men crucified with Jesus. Were there others? Which one is the man who became the Christ of faith?

If hundreds of scholars over more than three centuries cannot identify the historical man behind the religious figure we call Jesus, why should we assume that the Romans, who had lots of problems of their own, would do any better? Remember, two men were crucified

---

87   Wright, *Jesus and the Victory of God*, 472–473; White, *From Jesus to Christianity*, 35–39.

with Jesus. Which of the three was the Jesus of faith? Was Jesus there at all? Did the Romans ever get the right man?

The scholarly search for the historical person underlying the Christian gospel stories has yielded a maddening variety of often contradictory portraits. For Morton Smith, Jesus represented some sort of social magician; for Edward Schillebeeckx, Jesus proclaimed and instituted redemption for all Israel. D. E. P. Sanders regards Jesus as a Jewish prophet appointed to usher in the kingdom of God in conjunction with the destruction and rebuilding of the temple. Marcus Borg regards Jesus as standing in the charismatic tradition of Judaism, which cultivated an intense experience of spirit, and on it goes. Luke Timothy Johnson observed that the recent production of historical lives of Jesus has developed "images of Jesus that are remarkably diverse if not mutually incompatible."

"Whatever else the gospels were ... they were by and large not representational in the sense of reproducing the historical Jesus of the past." Wright seems to accept the gospel portrait of Jesus and regards him as the culmination of Israel's history, which was to recognize Jesus as the Messiah, restore Israel, and through a restored Israel, restore the world, defeat evil, and defeat death. John D. Crossan complains that the stunning variety of Jesus portraits "is an academic embarrassment."[88]

Jesus himself wrote nothing. We have no original copies of what the New Testament gospel writers record of what they had heard that Jesus had said or done. We do not even have copies of early copies. Prior to the nineteenth century, the earliest copies of

---

88   All of these scholars are cited in Werner H. Kelber, ed., *The Jesus Controversy* (Harrisburg, PA: Trinity Press International, 1999), 83–84.

New Testament manuscripts dated from the fourth century. In the twentieth century, we discovered some third-century fragments, but the discovery of earlier copies does not show that the copiers were particularly scrupulous about making an accurate reproduction of the text. These early texts were not really regarded, as Bart Ehrman puts it, "as the last word" on Jesus's teaching and deeds.[89] They were not seen as sacrosanct or inviolable until years after they first went into circulation. What we have are centuries of copies of copies of copies, and these copies all differ from one another, even when purportedly recording the same events.

There was, in short, no "orderly and uniform belief" in the early years of what became Christianity.[90] These early Christians were Jews trying to persuade their fellow Jews that the Jesus they preached was the culmination of their tradition. In his *Christianity without Fairy Tales*, Jim Rigas provides a half-page list of various Jesus followers.[91] When the gospel writers wrote their gospels, who were they quoting or watching? Jesus or someone who had seen or watched Jesus or a Jewish holy man who seemed to be saying things that were similar to those being said in the Jesus movement? Who said what they attribute to Jesus? According to Mark, there were no witnesses to the crucifixion. Jesus's followers all ran away. How can anyone be sure the Romans got the right man—the man who was later canonized as Jesus Christ? At this late date, how can we ever know?

Early Christianity was a cockpit of fiercely contending theologies. Bart Ehrman describes it well:

---

89   Ehrman, *Lost Christianities*, 49–50.
90   Rabbi Samuel Sandmel, *A Jewish Understanding of the New Testament*, 3rd ed. (Woodstock, VT: Skylight Paths, 2008), 34.
91   Rigas, *Christianity without Fairy Tales*, 241.

Imagine the choices facing Christians in the second century. Who is better: the Ebionite church or the Marcionite? Gnostic or proto-othodox? A church that believes in one God or twelve or thirty? A church that accepts the Gospels of Matthew, Mark, and Luke or the Gospels of Thomas, Philip and Mary? A church that believes God created the world or that the world is a cosmic mistake? A church that adheres to the Jewish laws of kashrut, Sabbath observance, and circumcision or a church that condemns these laws as inspired by an inferior deity?[92]

And this does not include the varying gnostic groups who infiltrated Christian churches well into the fourth century.

There were far more gospels circulating among early Christians than there are in the New Testament today. They circulated independently as separate gospels belonging to separate communities who had their own traditions and interpretations. We have no sure way of knowing what the original manuscripts said, who the gospel writers were, or who they were listening to as they wrote. Church leaders fought for centuries over which gospels would be included in the canon and which would be eliminated and destroyed, and which letters were in and which were out. The Bible as we know it today is the Bible of the clerics and churches who won the political struggle to control what was to be in the Bible. The successors of those clerics are today's mainline denominations and the Roman Catholic Vatican hierarchy, a hierarchy that now claims the exclusive power to determine what the Bible says and means.

---

92   Ehrman, *Lost Christianities*, 135.

We have already noted in chapter 2 that the God of the Hebrew Bible is an amalgam of different gods from different times and cultures[93] and that the stories of the Hebrew Bible were never intended to be "history" or "science" in the modern sense.[94] The problem may be worse in the New Testament, where what we have are gospels containing an amalgam of teachings from many sectarian Jewish movement leaders and where we can never be sure that the "Jesus" referred to is the Jesus of faith. Marcus Borg avoids the problem when he writes that the orthodox Christian doctrine of God is not an element of belief but an element of experience. God is the "sacred," "the spirit," and Jesus's relationship to the Spirit was the source of everything he was.

Note that Borg's analysis enables him to use conventional Christian images and language without having to defend the historical truth or probability of any of it. This is very clear when he uses the word *God* throughout when he really means an experience of the sacred. I asked him once why he went through all this if he did not really believe it. He replied that he could not dispense with the Christian traditions. When I asked if any other set of cultural symbols would do, he replied that he made no claim to exclusivity. There were many ways to speak of the "sacred."[95]

That may be, but it does not deal with the powerful diversity of what Borg has chosen to call "the sacred." Karen Armstrong ceased being a Catholic nun after seven miserable years and has since become a prolific religious writer. But despite "the greatest spiritual masters" who "insisted that God was not another being, and that

---

93 Miles, *God: A Biography*, 72.
94 Brettler, *How to Read the Jewish Bible*, 21–23, 38.
95 I was in the audience at Borg's lecture at the Harvard Episcopalian seminary when I asked these questions.

there was Nothing out there," she was "still seduced by the realistic supernatural theism that I thought I had left behind." She does not go to church. She belongs to no religious community. She writes prolifically and well on religious subjects. But, she writes, "I still live alone, spend my days in silence, and am wholly occupied in writing, thinking, and speaking about God and spirituality."[96]

John Dominic Crossan does not accept the divine conception of Jesus. Either all divine conceptions "from Alexander to Augustus and from Christ to the Buddha, should be accepted literally and miraculously or all of them should be accepted metaphorically and theologically." He does not believe that Jesus was bodily resurrected from the dead. He does not believe that Jesus raised Lazarus from the dead. Dead men cannot be brought back to life. He does not accept the story of the empty grave, which lies at the heart of Wright's resurrection argument. Jesus's bones probably wound up in a lime pit after they had been picked clean by wild animals, in accordance with the usual Roman practice.[97] Crossan believes none of the New Testament miracles but insists that he is a Christian and left the monastery and the priesthood but "not the Roman Catholic Church." What he appears to mean is that he retained something deeper than the institutional church: "a sacramental consciousness or embodied awareness that the holy appears through the profane if you can but see it."[98] Crossan believes that religious diversity is proof of religion's validity. People do not have religion as such; they have this religion or that religion, just as they speak this language

96   Karen Armstrong, *Up the Spiral Staircase* (New York: Anchor Books, 2004), 306.

97   Crossan, *The Birth of Christianity*, 28; Ibid., *Jesus: A Revolutionary Biography*, 2–20.

98   John Dominic Crossan, *A Long Way from Tipperary* (New York: HarperSanFrancisco, 2000), 97.

or that language. One way or the other, people seek meaning in life; they seek the "holy."[99]

A Protestant religious writer insists that "the Spirit" is always trying to communicate with us, and we should go to church because we are more likely to hear the Spirit's words in church than in a local bar. He concludes by writing: "I accept Christianity as the belief in the teachings of Jesus of Nazareth, as transmitted by the Evangelists, always keeping in mind that in the process some of them may have been altered or even completely fabricated. I reject the Nicene Creed in its entirety as an unsuccessful attempt by man to define and even describe God."[100] If that is the argument, Rigas should reject Paul's letters and the four Gospels as well.

The Anglican bishop N. T. Wright entitles his second volume on the New Testament *Jesus and the Victory of God*. God sent Jesus—theologically his son, but at the same time, theologically God—to defeat Satan, defeat evil, defeat death, and bring salvation to all mankind. But after Jesus was crucified, died, and was bodily resurrected after three days of death, nothing had changed! Wright ruefully concedes that "Jesus interpreted his coming death, and the vindication he expected after that death, as the defeat of evil; but on the first Easter Monday evil still stalked the earth from Jerusalem to Gibraltar and beyond." Nonetheless, writes Wright, while there was still some mopping up to do, early Christians, and presumably he himself, "believed that the real victory had been accomplished."[101] What was that victory?

---

99   Ibid., 100–101.
100   Rigas, *Christianity without Fairy Tales*, 343–344.
101   Wright, *Jesus and the Victory of God*, 659.

According to Luke Timothy Johnson, whatever sense of a new life Jesus's resurrection may have given is sadly missing now. The understanding of salvation as "good news has progressively weakened among professing Christians." In short, Jesus's ministry did not noticeably change the structures of society according to the measure of justice, and there is little evidence that lives changed.[102]

Even a conservative Trinitarian Christian like David Bentley Hart is unsure that Christianity has much influence now and thinks that post-Christian society may collapse into nihilism.[103] Nicolas Wade concludes simply that humanity has evolved with an instinct to be religious in order to enhance society's survival.[104] There is no evidence whatsoever that religion has ever helped a society survive or improved individual morality, but arguments that make belief in religion a natural element of human evolution essentially make religious doctrine and God irrelevant. The same is true of books that argue that the physical laws of the universe, mathematically expressed, are the language of God. But when the author finally succumbs to an overpowering urge to believe, he found, not an equation, but "the person of Jesus."[105] The language of God remains, as it always has been, silence.

---

102   Johnson, *The Creed*, 214.
103   David Bentley Hart, *Atheist Delusions* (New Haven and London: Yale University Press, 2009), 45, 107, 175–176, 206, and *passim*.
104   Wade, *The Faith Instinct*, 276.
105   Francis S. Collins, *The Language of God*, 220.

FOUR

ISLAM

The God of Islam revealed in the Koran is the God of the Bible as portrayed in the Jewish Old Testament and the Christian New Testament. The Koran also adopts many of the biblical stories that non-Islamic scholars have long since dismissed as pious fictions. In doing so, biblical scholars, of course, implicitly challenge the veracity of the Koran.[106] That raises an ancient dilemma in acute form: are we being addressed by the word of God or just another human being? For believing Muslims, the answer is made clear in an official statement of the Islamic faith prepared by the Islamic Affairs Department of the Saudi Arabian embassy in Washington, DC:

The Quran is a record of the exact words revealed by God through the angel Gabriel to the Prophet Muhammad. It was memorized by Muhammad and then dictated to his Companions,

---

106   Ibn Warraq, *Why I Am Not a Muslim* (Amherst, NY: Prometheus Books, 2003, 2005), 33; Han Küng, John Bowden, trans., *Islam: Past, Present & Future* (Oxford: One World, 2007, 2009), 412.

and written down by scribes who cross-checked it during his lifetime. Not one word of its 114 chapters, the Suras, has been changed over the centuries, so that the Quran is in every detail the unique and miraculous text which was revealed to Muhammad fourteen centuries ago.

The Quran, the last revealed Word of God, is the prime source of every Muslim's faith and practice.[107]

Compared to the treatment Jewish and Christian scriptures have received at the hands of biblical scholars, the Koran has been treated very gently. A major figure in Islamic scholarship, the late John Wansbrough, wrote: "As the record of Muslim revelation the book requires no introduction. As a document susceptible of analysis by the instruments and techniques of Biblical criticism it is virtually unknown."[108]

The Koran purports to "record the exact words revealed by God through the Angel Gabriel," but this is simply not so. Many of the revelations in the Koran are direct statements by Muhammad and are not from God. Even the opening sura of the Koran cannot be the word of God since it is a prayer addressed to God. Almost all editions of the Koran are in translation. Editors and translators solve the problem of transforming declarations by Muhammad into the words of God by inserting the word *say* in brackets at the beginning of a verse to give the appearance that Muhammad is merely reciting what God told him to say. They do this even when the original Arabic does not contain the word *say*.[109]

---

107 The Islamic Affairs Department (The Ambassy of Saudi Arabia, Washington, DC, 1989), 8.

108 John Wansbrough, Andrew Rippin, eds. and trans., *Quaranic Studies* (Amherst, NY: Prometheus Books, 2004), quoted from Rippin's introduction, xxi.

109 Warraq, *Why I Am Not a Muslim*, 106–107.

The phrase, "the last revealed Word of God," makes clear that Islam believes that there were Jewish and Christian revelations that were sent down by God before those recited by Muhammad. If Muhammad's "revelations" were to overcome the reverence that the Bible had accumulated over the centuries, they had to be established as the true word of God. When it was objected that there were no miracles sent to Muhammad by his lord, the Koran has God say: "'Say, Miracles lie in God's hands; I am here simply to warn you plainly.'" God then addresses Muhammad directly: "Do they not think it is enough that We have sent down the Scripture that is recited to them?"[110]

The Koran contains many stories of biblical figures from the Old and New Testaments, including Adam, Noah, Job, Moses, Abraham, Lot, Zachariah, Jesus, a few Arabian prophets, and, of course, Muhammad. But these stories are scattered, incomplete, and used in ways that are difficult to interpret. For example, "In God's eyes, Jesus is just like Adam: He created him from the dust, and said to him, 'Be' and he was."[111] This simply ignores the Old Testament, where Adam is the first man, and the New Testament, where Jesus is the son of God. The New Testament does not have Jesus made from dust; he is birthed by a woman. Moreover, it was Adam's disobedience that brought original sin. The Christian argument is that God sent Jesus to help mankind overcome that sin. But one can expect variations like this from an ongoing oral tradition.

Access to Bible stories was relatively easy in pre-Islamic Arabia. There was a widespread presence of Jewish Christianity, through

110 The Qur'an, trans. M. A. S. Abdel Hareem (Oxford: Oxford University Press, 2004, 2008) 29:50–51. From now on, I shall cite the Koran by sura and verse as above: 29:50–51.

111 Koran 3:59.

the Ebionites. In Jerusalem, the Ebionites had been led by James, the brother of Jesus. They were scattered into Arabia after the Roman destruction of Jerusalem in 70 CE. They were truly Jewish Christians. What separated them from their fellow Jews was their belief that Jesus was the promised Messiah and the divine son of God. Otherwise, they were thoroughly Jewish, traditionally monotheistic, and had been present in Arabia for six centuries before Muhammad started preaching. Many Arabs would have heard their stories.[112]

Indeed, the image of Muhammad that emerges from the Koran and traditional commentaries is extraordinarily reminiscent of Moses. The prophet does not bring down God's word carved on stone tablets; rather, the Koran rests on a stone table in heaven. In 1908, a scholar remarked that "Islam is nothing more nor less than Judaism plus the apostle-ship of Mohammad."[113] In 1987, the Protestant *Theologische Realenzyklopaedie* described Islam as a "syncretistic and eclectic collection of several religions from the world of Muhammad."[114] A more recent scholar writes that it is "indisputable and interesting" that the Koran incorporates Jewish and Christian sources and that some of the tales of the ancients found in the Koran "are not from canonical texts but from decidedly heterodox sources—the sorts of sources Muhammad would likely encounter in Arabia, where heretical Christianity predominated."[115]

Islam, therefore, recognizes Jews and Christians as "people of the book" who worship the same God who spoke to Muhammad through the angel Gabriel. However, the Jews and the Christians

---

112   Küng, *Islam*, 36–39.
113   S. M. Zwermer, quoted in Warraq, *Why I Am Not a Muslim*, 49.
114   Quoted in Küng, *Islam*, 61.
115   Robert Spencer, *The Truth about Muhammad* (Washington, DC: Regnery Publishing, Inc., 2006), 53.

deformed God's revelations, and Muhammad, "the seal of the prophets,"[116] was the messenger and last prophet who would bring them God's true and final revelation. The parallels with the Judeo-Christian story are patent: mankind goes wrong, and God sends the flood; mankind remains disobedient, and God sends prophet after prophet urging mankind to repent. He even sends Jesus, but to no avail.

Finally, God has to send the angel Gabriel to Muhammad to deliver his final revelation. Indeed, as the Koran tells the tale, Muhammad is very similar to Moses: he leads an exodus from Mecca to Medina; he delivers the word of God, which has been inscribed on a stone table in heaven; and even before the great conquests of his successors, he brings his people the promised land, Hijaz, which lies in Western Arabia. Despite these parallels, it is clear that Islam sees itself as a new, great monotheistic religion, separate and independent of Judaism and Christianity, and with its own sacred scripture, the Koran, as the final revelation. Traditional Islam is adamant that the Koran contains the eternal, unchanging word of God.

But even Muhammad conceded that in some circumstances, corrections of earlier revelations by later revelations were necessary. The Koran confirms this: "Any revelation We cause to be superseded or forgotten, We replace with something better or similar."[117] Muhammad is said to have recited revelations for almost twenty years, and scholars have estimated that there are anywhere from two to five hundred abrogations in the Koran—that is, suras or verses that replace or amend earlier ones. How can that be if the Koran contains the unchanging word of God, taken from a holy book

---

116   Koran 33:40.
117   Koran, 2:106; Küng, *Islam*, 118–119.

that has lain unchanged in heaven on its stone table or tablet for all eternity? Why would an all-knowing and all-powerful God have to change his mind so many times?[118]

This created great difficulties for Muhammad's followers. Since the suras of the Koran were not assembled in chronological order, but in order of length, with the longest suras coming first and the shortest last, no one knew where or when Muhammad had recited his revelations. No one could reconstruct the chronology of the suras after Muhammad died. How could anyone tell which sura came first and was later abrogated or amended? Which was the original sura, and which the corrected sura? When the Koran is recited, whether in services, from minarets calling the faithful to services, in prayer, or by schoolchildren memorizing all or parts of the Koran, error is being proclaimed as well as the word of God.

Jewish and Christian biblical criticism have had virtually no impact on the Koran. All the biblical stories it incorporates are presented in what non-Muslim scholars have long referred to as the precritical style, as if they were historical events related by God. Abraham and Ishmael built the Ka'Aba in Mecca. Noah and his family sailed on the ark. A man named Moses actually led the Jews on the exodus from Egypt and received the Pentateuch from God at Mount Sinai. A man named Jonah spent time in the belly of a whale.

In the Koran, an angel says: "Mary, God gives you news of a Word from Him, whose name will be the Messiah, Jesus, son of Mary, who will be held in honour in this world and the next, who will be one of those brought near to God."[119] The Gospel of Luke has a similar

---

118   Warraq, *Why I Am Not a Muslim*, 114–115.
119   Koran 3:45–46.

story of an angel telling Mary that God has favored her with a son to be named Jesus: "He shall be great and shall be called the son of the Highest."[120] The Koran also states that Jesus was not crucified: "though it was made to appear like that to them ... God raised him up to Himself. God is almighty and wise." The Koran never questions the historicity of Jesus. Indeed, the Koran and presumably Islam accept all the biblical figures and events as historical fact.[121]

The Koran insists that Muhammad was illiterate in order to make it clear that Muhammad was only reciting the words of God and not merely plagiarizing Jewish and Christian scriptures. Muhammad was often met with comments like, "We have heard all this before—we could say something like this if we wanted ... This is nothing but ancient fables," or "We have heard such promises before, and so did our forefathers. These are just ancient fables."[122] Muhammad's illiteracy was supposed to confirm that he was merely a messenger of God.

To Jewish and Christian listeners who challenged Muhammad to convert to their faiths, the Koran instructs Muhammad to say: "'No, [ours is] the religion of Abraham, the upright, who did not worship any God beside God." Muhammad is further instructed to tell his listeners: "We believe in God and in what was sent down to us and what was sent down to Abraham, Ishmael, Isaac, Jacob, and the Tribes, and what was given to Moses, Jesus, and all the prophets by their Lord. We make no distinction between any of them, and we devote ourselves to Him."[123] Muhammad wanted very much to convert Jews and Christians and would declaim: "How can you

120   Luke 1:28–32ff.
121   Koran 4:157–158; Warraq, *Why I Am Not a Muslim*, 144–147.
122   Koran 8:31, 23:83; Spencer, *The Truth about Muhammad*, 50–52, 47ff.
123   Koran 2:135–136.

argue with us about God when He is our Lord and your Lord?" In a peculiar passage where God seems to wonder if Muhammad is being rejected because the Old Testament is not Islamic, God has Muhammad ask: "Are you saying that Abraham, Ishmael, Jacob, and the Tribes were Jews or Christians?" Muhammad is then instructed to answer his own question: "Who knows better: you or God?"[124] The Koran is not always crystal clear.

Muhammad says repeatedly that devout, monotheistic Jews and Christians should be respected as "people of the book," but they must now abide by the rules of the Islamic community. These passages and others never leave it entirely clear where Jews and Christians stood if they did not convert but remained devout and pious within their own traditions. The general practice was that the non-Muslims paid a special tax but could continue to exercise their religion.

For the non-Muslim historian, the traditional histories of Muhammad and the rise of Islam in the seventh century verge on myth. There may have been a Muhammad, but we know nothing about him. He must have been a man with considerable charisma as well as a successful tribal leader of the powerful Qurayish tribe, who led them to several important victories. Gods had to be victorious over the enemy to be successful. Only the Jews had a God who gave them no victories. Muhammad is said to have died in 632, but we have no biography of Muhammad, no commentary on the Koran, no reliable accounts of what Muhammad said and did, no documents on the history of early Islam, and no early law books making any reference to a Koran. No documents at all on Islam or Muhammad existed in the form in which we now have them earlier than the ninth century.[125]

---

124 Koran 2:139–140.
125 Ibn Warraq, *What the Koran Really Says* (Amherst, NY: Prometheus Books, 2002), 89, citing G. G. Hawting and John Wansbrough.

As a source on the life of the prophet, the Koran is useless. It was meant to relay the word of God, not outline the life of the prophet. Given the fragmentary and often incoherent nature of the Koranic text, early Muslim scholars developed a body of commentary on the Koran, called *tafsir*, and a huge corpus of traditions relating to what the prophet said and did, called Hadith. Together, these two bodies of traditional commentary make up the Sunna, or model of the prophet, all of which were written more than a century after Muhammad died. The Sunna is regarded by most Muslims as second only to the Koran in authority even though many of them admit that a great many of the Hadith are forged. Many Hadith authors tried to date their Hadith back to the time of Muhammad to enhance its authority.

About a century after Muhammad's death, a biography of the prophet, the Sira, was put together from the Hadith and the Koran. Unfortunately, the original form of this biography is lost to us, and the shorter version put together afterward is so uncritically hagiographical that its accuracy is "questionable."[126] None of this literature was reduced to writing until at least a century after Muhammad's death, but it is what Muslim tradition is based upon.

That tradition claims that an Arab businessman in Mecca, born about 570, a member of the powerful Quraysh tribe of that city, received his first revelation from God through the angel Gabriel in 610, and began preaching publicly in 613. Muslim tradition also holds that Muhammad was illiterate. He could not write down the revelations; all he could do was recite a revelation when it was delivered to him to whomever was in earshot, at first to family and close friends and then to others. Listeners committed the revelations to memory or wrote them

---

126 Spencer, *The Truth About Muhammad*, 24–28.

down on whatever scraps of wood, bone, leather, or stone they had at hand. Muhammad himself is said to have committed many revelations to memory, although even he admitted that he could have forgotten some verses, that self-deception was possible, that the "devil" could sometimes distort God's revelation, and that in some circumstances, corrections of earlier revelations might be necessary.[127]

The original religious movement that Muhammad founded and led was a monotheistic movement whose members called themselves "the Believers." It is out of this movement that Islam developed. Scholars have argued that there is a considerable body of Arab religious texts dating from the first century and a half of Arab rule that is demonstrably not Islam. There is no reference to Muhammad or the prophet in Arab religious institutions prior to 691 CE.[128] The Believers' message was simple: there is no God but God. "He is the originator of the heavens and the earth, and when He decrees something, He says only, 'Be,' and it is." God acts alone. He had no child. He needs no helpers. Many Western scholars have treated this early movement as a religious cover for raiding parties seeking expansion and loot. Fred M. Donner thinks otherwise. He argues that Muhammad was an inspired visionary who claimed to be a prophet receiving revelations from God, and since many people of the Near East were already close to being monotheists, Donner believes that Muhammad's original "Believers" movement can "best be characterized as a monotheistic reform movement, rather than a new and distinct religious confession."[129]

---

127 Koran 2:106; Küng, *Islam*, 118–119.
128 See Zehuda D. Nevo, "Towards A Prehistory of Islam" in Warraq, *What the Koran Really Says*, 132–133. There are a number of scholars who believe Yehuda D. Nevo is dating the origins of Islam far too late. That may be true, but we really know very little about the origins of Islam.
129 Fred M. Donner, *Muhammad and the Believers* (Cambridge, MA: The Belknap Press of Harvard University Press, 2010), 53, 86–87.

Believers were expected to reject polytheism and believe in one God, prayer, pious behavior, compassion, fasting, and pilgrimage. They were also expected to believe in a last judgment when the dead would be raised from their graves to face God. Piety, fasting, and pilgrimages were not new; they were existing polytheistic practices. The pilgrimage to the Ka'Aba in Mecca had long been a pagan rite. According to Genesis, Abraham and Ishmael[130] built the Ka'Aba as the house of God; the polytheistic tribes of Arabia used it to house their idols. In 630, once he had gained control of Mecca, Muhammad had the idols removed and the Ka'Aba became, as was the Israelite holy of holies, the sacred house of God. Like the polytheist pagans before them, Muslims continued the practice of circumambulating the Ka'Aba as an act of worship.

The beliefs and practices of the Believers and later, early Islam devotees, were not new to the two great monotheistic traditions of that time, although Christians might have been shocked by Muhammad's rejection of Jesus as the crucified and resurrected son of God. The Arabians did not yet have a solid monotheistic religion or a holy scripture, like the Jews and the Christians. If Arabia, squeezed between the Byzantine and the Sasanian Persian Empires, had not been united by its own great religion, it would have collapsed into an impoverished mass of squabbling tribes. The Koran says that as Abraham and Ishmael built the Ka'Ba, they pleaded with God to raise up a messenger who would "teach them from the Scripture and wisdom and purify them: You are the Mighty, the Wise."[131]

Muhammad, the Believers, and the Koran were therefore fiercely monotheistic. Polytheism was the enemy, including Christianity, if

---

130   Genesis 13:18; Koran 2:125.
131   Koran, 2:129.

its adherents insisted upon a trinity in which Jesus was the divine son of God. Traditional Muslim narratives and modern scholars routinely refer to Muhammad and his followers as "Muslims." But Muhammad and his followers referred to themselves as "Believers." The Koran addresses itself overwhelmingly to "Believers," not "Muslims."[132] It was not until the eighth century that Islam began to coalesce from the Believers movement into a clearly defined and distinct religious confession.[133] Later, Muslim commentary consistently translates "Believer" as "Muslim" to give Islam the legitimacy of an old tradition.

After Muhammad's death, Believers feared that the revelations committed to memory would be forgotten and that the bits and pieces of revelation that were written down would be lost. There are several traditional accounts about how the Koran was put together. The Islamic Affairs Department of the Saudi Arabian embassy in Washington argues for a Koran that was assembled and finalized as we have it today during Muhammad's lifetime. That is a highly controversial statement and does not seem to be a position that has wide support among non-Islamic scholars.

According to Islamic tradition, Muhammad died in 632. He got his first revelation in 610. He started public preaching in 613. This means that in less than twenty-two years, he assembled and canonized the holy scripture of a major monotheistic religion while struggling for recognition as God's spokesman against the hostility of his own polytheistic tribe in Mecca. During this brief period, he moved to Medina with loyal followers, struggled to consolidate his political position there, raided Meccan caravans to raise money, and

---

132   Koran, see the bracketed inserts at 2:136 and 137.
133   Donner, *Muhammad and the Believers*, 111–112.

fought several wars. If Muhammad was reciting, assembling, and editing the eternal word of God during this period, he must have done it in his spare time.

Fred Donner notes that this picture of Muhammad's early career "is not drawn from documents or even stories dating from Muhammad's time, but from literary sources that were compiled many years—sometimes centuries—later." They are not reliable accounts of what happened, "but are rather legends created by later generations of Muslims to affirm Muhammad's status as a prophet." These concerns have led some scholars to conclude that the traditional Islamic commentaries are worthless as historical sources. Donner thinks that is going too far; he believes there are some nuggets of truth to be found there but admits it is difficult to tell fact from fiction in that kind of literature.[134] Robert Spencer, a writer who is fairly hostile to Islam, goes even further: "From a strictly historical point of view, it is impossible to state with certainty that a man named Muhammad actually existed, or if he did, that he did much or any of what is ascribed to him."[135]

Sources for the assembly of the Koran are equally unreliable, but if we reject the traditional accounts, argues Donner, "we are left unsure just what kind of text the Quran is and where it came from."[136] Jewish and Christian biblical scholars face similar problems but have developed analytical techniques that enable them to get closer to original sources. Islam is hampered by the dogma that the Koran is an eternal and therefore uncreated book that cannot be treated historically.

---

134   Donner, *Muhammad and the Believers*, 50–52 and 50ff.
135   Spencer, *The Truth about Muhammad*, 31.
136   Donner, *Muhammad and the Believers*, 54.

Traditional stories of the Koran's assembly into a book are many and confused and tell of followers who tried to put together private collections of the revelations into codex form. As Islam spread, collections of Muhammad's revelations, known as the Metropolitan Codices, appeared in centers like Mecca, Medina, Damascus, Kufa, and Basra. Usually, the revelations were collected in chapters, called suras, which were themselves divided into verses. According to traditional Muslim history, the Caliph Uthman (644–656) tried to bring order to this chaos of allegedly Koranic texts by appointing a team of Muhammad's companions led by Muhammad's personal secretary to have the various fragments and memories of revelation collected, edited, and put in codex form as a single, unified text that is now called the Uthman Codex. Caliph Uthman sent copies of the codices to all the metropolitan centers along with orders that they be used in place of copies that until then had been considered to be authentic. Uthman also ordered that all earlier copies be burned.[137] That left the Uthman Codex as the only officially valid Koranic scripture in the Muslim world.

According to Muslim tradition, this Uthman Codex was immediately accepted as the word of God, just as it had been delivered to Muhammad by the angel Gabriel. It has come down through the centuries without a single word being changed. The codex was probably completed by Uthman's death in 656, or shortly thereafter. Despite Uthman's orders to destroy all other versions of the Koran, there have always been variant versions in the Muslim world. In 1923, Egypt made the Uthman edition of the Koran the standard edition, and that is the edition accepted by most orthodox Muslims today. It is impossible to tell whether the Egyptian standard edition of 1923 is the seventh-century Uthman Codex. Its lineage is far too confused.

---

137   Ibid., 153–154.

Since Muhammad died in 632 and Caliph Uthman in 656, the Uthman tradition that the Saudi embassy in Washington, DC, adopted requires us to believe that within twenty or thirty years of the prophet's death, the scattered Koranic texts were collected, the oral traditions committed to writing, the limits of the Koran defined, and the Uthman Codex accepted as the final canon of Islam's most sacred scripture: the Koran. Donner puts the final assembly of the revelations into a Koran at "about twenty years after Muhammad's death"—at least, Donner believes, "all the Quran text is demonstrably early."[138] So does Tarif Khalid, who asserts that we can be confident that the present Koran is the Uthman text of 650 CE. Given the many centuries it took the Jews to fix the canon for their Bible and that the canon for Christianity was not fixed until well into the fourth century,[139] this canonization took place with almost blinding speed.

That speed troubles a number of scholars. Andrew Rippen, in his introduction to the 2004 reprint of John Wansbrough's *Quaranic Studies*, writes that if we are to have a meaningful discussion of the Koran, "three elements must come into play: one, there must be a fixed body of text that is, two, written down, and, three, has some measure of acceptance among a group of people as a source of authority." Rippen suggests that there are "tensions" within the Muslim community's account of the collection of the Koran. For example, the tribes of Arabia spoke a number of tribal dialects of Arabic while the Koran claims it is written in a "pure" Arabic that scholars have called Classic Arabic. We have no evidence that Classic Arabic existed before the Koran, nor do we even know what "Classic Arabic" might have consisted of at that time. According to

---

138   Ibid., 54–55.
139   Armstrong, *The Bible*, 66.

Andrew Rippen and other scholars, "the emergence of a fixed and explicit script for the Arabic language suggests a considerably longer time frame than the community's account, on its surface, seems to allow." The process of text formation was a long one, and the notion of a fixed Koran "existing under Uthman ... is quite anachronistic." When and how did religious leaders and the common people come to recognize the Koran as sacred scripture? "This stage of recognition cannot be pinned down; it does not happen overnight as a result of one person's actions or even the actions of a group of people."[140]

The whole tradition of a seventh-century Uthman Codex is suspect. None of the early literature on the Koran presupposes the existence of a standard fixed text as early as the seventh century, and there is no reference to such a canon anywhere where one would expect it to appear, such as records of court proceedings or arbitrations or serious family disputes. We simply do not have the information to ascertain how the canon of the Koran was determined. How long did it take? Where did it take place? Who made the final decisions? Given the evidence, is the Koran to be fully attributed to Muhammad? How were the limits of the canon text determined? Is there evidence that the Koran was reformulated, added to, changed, or developed during the process of canonization?[141] Donner thinks there was. The Koran claims to be in a "clear Arab tongue," but many passages remain far from clear "even in the most basic sense of knowing what the words might have meant in the original context." The Koran shows evidence of including older texts that have been reused and revised. Styles in different parts of the Koran differ "markedly." The Koran, indeed, may be a text that is a composite of originally separate texts hailing from different communities.[142]

---

140   Andrew Rippen, *Wansbrough's Quaranic Studies*, "Forward," xiv–xvi.
141   Ibid., xviii.
142   Donner, *Muhammad and the Believers*, 56.

We do not know. The late John Wansbrough, for example, argued "that the structure itself of Muslim scripture lends little support to the theory of a deliberate edition." The structure of the text does not reflect a carefully executed project of one or of many men, but rather, "the product of an organic development from originally independent traditions during a long period of transmission."[143] The dogma of an eternal, uncreated Koran that fell from heaven and into Muhammad's heart is another one of those miracles that is supposed to establish scripture as the word of God, but it constitutes a serious obstacle for a critical analysis of the Koran.[144]

Uthman's order to destroy all versions of the Koran earlier than his was never effective. The problem was that the language of the Koran, like the Hebrew of the Jewish text, is consonantal and a number of variant versions of the text survived well after the year 1000. The consonants might be identical from text to text, but you could not tell which letter any given consonant was until the proper diacritical marks were made to differentiate them. Special marks were also required to indicate where vowels were to be used, and that also influenced what a given word might mean and how it was to be read. Finally, a number of consonantal texts came down that were simply unmarked. As a result, a number of variant readings were possible depending upon how the distinguishing marks and dots were added and interpreted. After several centuries, it was impossible to tell how the original Uthman text had been marked, or pointed, and literally thousands of variant readings of particular verses existed, making it difficult to know what the true original form had been. By 935, there was a definite canonization of one system of consonants and a limit was placed on the variation of vowels used in a text. This resulted

---

143 Wansbrough, *Quranic Studies*, 47.
144 Küng, *Islam*, 52, 67.

in a total of seven acceptable variant readings, but other scholars accepted ten and still others accepted fourteen readings. At present, two systems seem to be in use, the main one being the standard Egyptian edition of 1923, which gained a kind of official status by virtue of being adopted as the standard edition by Egypt.[145]

The Koran is now the sacred text of Islam. But the Koran is an extraordinarily opaque book. Even apart from the intellectual hurdle of accepting the text of it as the uncreated and unchanging word of God, the Koran is often incomprehensible. What does the holy scripture of Islam say? There are words and suras that have multiple meanings. In which language did Muhammad recite his revelations and in which language was the Koran originally assembled? There are many words and phrases whose meanings have still not been recovered. There are many interpolations where the authors blended tribal dialects with a purer Arabic.

Early Muslims were aware of the many contradictions and ambiguities in the Koran and developed mountains of commentary, the Hadith, to explain them. But no existing Hadith can be reliably attributed to the prophet. The usual Muslim argument is that reading and rereading the Koran makes its message clearer, but the plain fact is that at least one-fifth of the Koran is completely, and perhaps hopelessly, incomprehensible. One out of five sentences simply make no sense; they are neither readable nor translatable. Some verses in the suras are clear, and some are ambiguous, and no one but God knows how to interpret them. Muslim doctrine states that the Koran is written and was delivered to Muhammad in pure, clear Arabic. But the current text is not pure, clear Arabic; it contains foreign words

---

145 Warraq, *Why I Am Not a Muslim*, 108–110. This paragraph is a highly condensed paraphrase of Warraq's excellent account of the difficulties in Koranic textual analysis.

and words that no one understands. The Koran would be totally incomprehensible without glossaries and entire commentaries. "Even the most educated of Arabs will need some sort of translation if he or she wishes to make sense" of the Koran.[146]

Ibn Warraq, who has written several angry and critical books on Islamic traditions, can barely contain his rage at conservative scholars who seem to believe there is an "authentic" Koran out there without offering any sensible account of how or when that Koran came into being. How "do they think Muhammad received his 'revelations'?" he asks.

Do they believe that Muhammad literally went into a trance and somehow saw visions of angels who recited various verses to him, which he then revealed to his companions, who then wrote them down verbatim? Some of the passages and stories in the Quran are very long indeed. Are we to understand that Muhammad remembered several hundred lines of rhymed prose that were "revealed" to him in his trance? Do we assume that all his companions were literate, and able to write down every word, all the time believing that their prophet was in direct communion with an angel?

What about the various Judaic and Christian elements that have gone into the making of the Koran? From which Koran are we working? There are dozens of different translations in the bookstores. "Neither Western scholars nor ordinary Muslims have, it seems, something called the Quran, they all make do with a Quran."[147] The result is that we now have a situation "that in the twenty-first

---

146 Warraq, *What the Koran Really Says*, 26.
147 Ibid., 92.

century we still do not have a definitive, scholarly text of the Quran." Ibn Warraq adds that "there never has been a definitive text of this holy book."[148]

As mentioned above, according to orthodox Islamic tradition, the revelations from God came to Muhammad in a pure, clear Arabic and Muhammad recited the revelations in this pure form of Arabic, called Classic Arabic. "Truly, this Qur'an has been sent down by the Lord of the Worlds ... in a clear Arabic tongue." That cannot be true. Classic Arabic, also known as Koranic Arabic, came into use as a literary language in the seventh to ninth centuries and became a sacred language because of its use in the Koran. It did not become a stabilized language in Muhammad's lifetime, and there are still words in the Koran that no one understands.

Moreover, the majority of Muslims are not Arabic-speaking, and modern Arab populations do not speak, read, or even think in Classic Arabic. Very few speakers from any Arab country can really speak Arabic. Muhammad must have heard the revelations in Quraysh, the dialect of his tribe, and that must have been the early language of the Koran—but the fact is that we do not have the slightest idea in which language Muhammad received his revelations or recited them or in which language the early Koran was written. If, as is likely, Muhammad recited his revelations in the Quraysh dialect and the Koran now has an Arabic text, then someone committed the blasphemy of changing the unchanging word of God.

Fred Donner believes that one reason that Islam spread so rapidly and with relatively little violence was that the Near East was already moving toward monotheism or, at least, was very ready to accept it.

---

148   Warraq, *Why I Am Not Muslim*, 108.

Most of the tribes and towns were not being forced to accept new doctrine. All the Believers asked was that they adopt monotheism and pay tribute. The tribes and cities were probably already paying tribute to former masters, the Byzantines or the Sasanian Empire.

During the early years of the Umayad Dynasty, which lasted until 750 CE, the Caliphs were absorbed in their huge conquests, fights over the spoils, and the succession of the caliphate. They displayed little enthusiasm for religion and ignored the fact that most Arabs were so ignorant of the Koran that one could recite them almost anything without their having the slightest idea whether what was being recited was the word of God or not.[149]

What is clear is that Muhammad used revelations of God's eternal word to settle family matters, personal quarrels, and difficulties with his wives and concubines. In sura 111, for example, Muhammad has God curse an uncle, one Abu Lahab, who had long been a bitter opponent of his: "May the hand of Abu Lahab be ruined! May he be ruined too ... He will burn in the Flaming Fire—and so will his wife." This is surely much too personal to be part of God's last revelation to mankind and shows once again that the Koran is in need of the serious higher criticism that seared the Jewish and Christian traditions.

It is always the same. This God, who is never seen, always ineffable, and eternally unknowable, speaks to anonymous Middle Eastern nomads, a Palestinian peasant no one had ever heard of, and an Arab merchant who could equally well be a typical tribal raider or God's last prophet. And if you disbelieve the messenger, you "will

149   Warraq, *What the Koran Really Says*, 80; Warraq, *Why I Am Not a Muslim*, 70.

be fuel for Hell: that is where you will go." "Those who have rejected the Truth will be led to Hell in their throngs." They will burn for all eternity. If they thirst, they will be given boiling water. No wonder Rabbi Soloveitchik is in despair over a God that disappears at the very moment that the rabbi turns to look for him for solace.

A recent book on religion argues that religion is an evolutionary phenomenon that makes communities more cohesive, efficient, and able to survive. As long as the religion performs these functions effectively, there is no particular need for a god, nor does it make any difference which god or scripture is followed.[150] This was precisely the attitude of ancient polytheism: if the chosen god did not bring success in war or the hunt and preserve the community, it was replaced.

The Mormons have learned a lot from polytheism.

---

150   Nicholas Wade, *The Faith Instinct*.

FIVE

THE MORMONS

God has to make contact with human beings to make his will known. The sheer antiquity, power, and richness of the Pentateuch has enabled it to shape the Jewish Old Testament. The Christian New Testament depends entirely upon the Jewish Old Testament. The Koran of Islam draws heavily upon Jewish and Christian traditions. And now, we have the twentieth-century Book of Mormon of Joseph Smith, Jr.[151] The introduction to the Book of Mormon states that it was written on plates of gold and records the history of two great civilizations. One came from Jerusalem in 600 BCE and afterward separated into two nations, the Nephites and the Lamanites. The second civilization, the Jaredites, came much earlier at the time of the Tower of Babel. "After thousands of years, all were destroyed except the Lamanites, and they are the principal

151   Joseph Smith, Jun., trans., *The Book of Mormon* (Salt Lake City: The Church of Jesus Christ of Latter-Day Saints, 1981 ed., printed in the United States, 2002). For reasons known only to himself, Joseph Smith, Jr., always wrote "Jun." instead of "Jr."

ancestors of the American Indians." The introduction invites all men who read The Book of Mormon "to ponder in their hearts the message it contains, and then to ask God, the Eternal Father, in the name of Christ if the book is true." This immediately introduces a recurrent religious problem: are we dealing with God or the words of human beings?

In the Jewish tradition, God spoke through Abraham, Noah, Moses, and the prophets. In the Christian tradition, God spoke through Jesus. In the Muslim tradition, God spoke through the angel Gabriel, who whispered into Muhammad's ear, and Muhammad then recited God's revelations. Muhammad's revelations are now collected in the Koran. In the Mormon tradition, God spoke to the fourteen-year-old Joseph Smith, Jr., as he was walking through the woods in upstate New York, and it was Joseph Smith who eventually produced The Book of Mormon, claiming that it had been given to him by God.

The sole doctrinal basis of the Mormon Church—officially the Church of Jesus of Latter-Day Saints—is the claim of Joseph Smith, Jr., that God revealed himself to him in a vision while he was walking in the woods at the age of fourteen. Scripture, for Mormons, includes: (1) The Book of Mormon, discovered and translated by Joseph Smith; (2) the *Pearl of Great Price*, Joseph Smith's own translation of ancient Egyptian papyri, which he purchased from a man who was touring the area showing Egyptian mummies and papyri; (3) Smith's adaptation of the King James Bible; and (4) a collection of revelations and declarations called *Doctrine and Covenants*, which purports to record the revelations of God to Joseph.

Mormons believe in what they call an "open canon," that is, that God continuously reveals himself through time, as he did with

Muhammad. Only the Mormon leader who bears the title "seer, prophet, and revelator" or first president, receives God's revelations. One hundred and thirty-three of the one hundred and thirty-eight revelations collected in *Doctrine and Covenants* were revelations to Joseph Smith. Finally, although it does not have quite the formal status of these three books, there is Joseph Smith's "King Follett Discourse," a sermon he delivered on April 7, 1844, which added major elements to Mormon beliefs. Since Joseph Smith wrote (or "translated") The Book of Mormon and the *Pearl of Great Price*, personally adapted the King James Bible for use by the church, and delivered the "King Follett Discourse," the Mormon Church's sacred documents are essentially the words of Joseph Smith,[152] just as the Koran consists of the words of Muhammad.

Joseph Smith, Jr., was born in Vermont on December 23, 1805, but was raised in Palmyra, New York, where his family moved when he was nine years old. That part of western New York state was known as the "Burned-Over District" because of the extraordinary number of churches, religious movements, and hell-fire-and-damnation revivalists active in the area. Apart from the revivalists, there were dozens of prophets who had visions and claimed to speak for God, such as Ann Lee, founder of the Shakers. Among the more traditional religions, there were Presbyterians and Quakers; the Methodists, who split four ways between 1814 and 1830; and the Baptists who split into Reformed Baptists, Hard-Shell Baptists, Free-

---

152 The account of the Mormon Church and Joseph Smith that follows, I took from: Fawn M. Brodie, *No Man Knows My History* (New York: Vintage Books Ed., Random House, 1995); Richard N. Ostling and Joan K. Ostling, *Mormon America: The Power and the Promise* (San Francisco: HarperSanFrancisco, 1999); Stephan Prothero, *American Jesus* (New York: Farrar, Strauss, and Giroux, 2003), the chapter on Mormonism, 162ff.; and C. Clark Julius, *Joseph Smith* (The Philalethes, August 1987), a pamphlet downloaded from Google: "Joseph Smith, Jr.").

Will Baptists, Seventh-Day Baptists, and Footwashers.[153] Palmyra was then a typical frontier area where people moved in, bought land, tried to make ends meet, and were often bought out or foreclosed on and moved on. It was an ever-changing population, and there were few stable institutions. As a social and religious milieu, it was much like first-century Palestine and seventh-century Arabia.

Joseph's adolescent world seethed with movement, religious passion, prophets, and con artists. The line between religion and magic was never very clear. His parents were devout; they prayed and read the Bible at home, but they were not attached to any church. They instilled in young Joseph a faith in Jesus and an interest in the Bible but insisted that he make his religious choice on his own. Official Mormon history portrays a religious but troubled adolescent who wanted to be saved but did not know where to turn until he had his vision in 1820.[154] That may be, but Joseph himself confessed on several occasions that he spent much of his adolescence learning the techniques of searching out water and treasure with divining rods and "seer stones." He was an uneducated, amiable young man and a famously engaging storyteller with a gift for fantasy and an extraordinary imagination. He was known to embed almost any incident or anecdote within a vast, imaginary world filled with kings, spirits, and wonderful events in which he usually played the leading role. Non-Mormons have argued all along that Joseph never had a vision in 1820 at all. He just made up the story of his vision years later to give The Book of Mormon authority as the true word of God.

The official version of Joseph's religious experience goes as follows. In 1820, when he was fourteen, Joseph was walking in the

---

153   Brodie, *No Man*, 12–13; Ostling, *Mormon America*, 20–22.

154   The details of Joseph Smith's adolescence are from Julius; Prothero, 167–170; Brodie, *No Man Knows My History*, 16–33.

woods alone, when two persons appeared in a brilliantly white pillar of light. Joseph dictated at least three different versions of this first vision between 1831 or 1832 and 1839. In Joseph's earliest version, Jesus alone appeared to him, but in the canonical version, written in 1938 and now used by the Mormon Church, there were two "Personages, whose brightness and glory defy all description."[155] One of them called Joseph by name, pointed to the other, and said, "This is my beloved Son. Hear him!" The fourteen-year-old Joseph asked for guidance: Which church should he join? According to the canonized version of Joseph's account, "I was answered that I must join none of them, for they were all wrong; and the Personage who addressed me said that all their creeds were an abomination in his sight; that those professors were all corrupt."[156] There is no record of Joseph having told anyone about his vision at the time. Why would anyone pay attention to a fourteen-year-old who claimed to have met Jesus while walking in the woods? Why would anyone believe that Jesus had told *him* that the creeds of all existing churches were an "abomination in his sight"? That vision could have been a dream, another one of his stories, a barely remembered flight of imagination, or it might never have happened. Mormon literature always refers to Joseph's claim as the "First Vision."[157]

Three years after the First Vision, when he was seventeen, Smith had a second vision. This too began with a blinding light, and this time, a single figure appeared in an "exceedingly white and brilliant" robe. The figure identified himself as the angel Moroni, a member of an ancient race and a messenger sent by God to tell young Joseph that there "was a book deposited, written upon gold plates, giving an account of the former inhabitants of this continent and the sources

---

155   Quoted in Prothero, *American Jesus*, 170.
156   Ibid., 170–171.
157   Prothero, *American Jesus*, 170.

from which they sprang. Moroni also said that the fullness of the everlasting Gospel was contained in the book, as delivered by the Savior to the ancient inhabitants."[158] In the official version of this story, Moroni tells Joseph to inform his father, and the elder Smith assures his son that Moroni's words are the true word of God. Joseph later claimed that he then led his father to the spot where Moroni had said the golden Bible was buried in a stone box. Sure enough, there was the stone box! But the angel Moroni warned that Joseph was not spiritually mature enough to take the plates. He would be told when he was ready for God's new message.

Around this time, an itinerant magician came through the area and claimed that he could locate water near the surface and treasure buried by the Indians. The magician had several magic stones, so-called "seer stones," which he looked into to locate the water and buried treasure. Joseph was fascinated. He watched the man work the area, collected several stones of his own, and claimed to have used them to locate some lost tools. Joseph and his father became active in using divining rods and magic stones to find buried treasure. This activity was known as "digging" and was illegal when done for pay. There is no record that Joseph or his father ever found any treasure, but young Joseph seems to have acquired a reputation as something of an adept. In any event, he and his father were hired by a group of treasure hunters for three dollars a day. Joseph used to put his "seer stones" in his hat, stick his face into the hat, and wait until the stones told him where the water or treasure lay. Needless to say, the diggers found nothing, the group broke up angrily, and in the spring of 1826, the former treasure hunters brought charges of fraud and disorderly conduct. Joseph was found guilty, but there is no record of the sentence imposed.[159]

---

158   Ibid., 171; Ostling, 24.
159   Julius, *Joseph Smith.*

During the course of this treasure hunting, Joseph fell in love with one digger's daughter, Emma Hale. Emma's father regarded Joseph as a lazy, arrogant fraud and opposed the match. Emma defied her father and married Joseph anyway, after which they lived with Joseph's parents in Palmyra, New York.

Finally, on September 27, 1827, Joseph declared that Moroni had permitted him to take "temporary" possession of the plates. These, Joseph claimed, were thin sheets of gold, bound in three rings. Joseph said the writing on the plates was Egyptian—well, not exactly Egyptian, but a kind of "reformed Egyptian," which had to be translated. Two "seer stones" came with the book to enable Joseph to make the translation.

Joseph took the golden book home. He would not let his wife or his parents see it. He hung a blanket across the room, went behind it, sat at a table, put his magic stones in his hat, thrust his face into the hat, and began dictating to his wife, Emma, who sat on the other side of the blanket. Joseph explained that he had to cover his face with his hat so that he could keep out all extraneous light and translate by looking at the stones.[160] When Emma grew tired, she was assisted by a prosperous farmer from the Palmyra area who was enthralled by Joseph's story. Joseph later had to call in more scribes. All of them sat on the other side of the blanket as they wrote down his dictation. No one was allowed to see the plates. Joseph kept them in a box, covered by a blanket, and translated them into English by gazing into the magic stones.

Emma's father came to visit, expecting to see his son-in-law working to support his daughter. Instead, he saw Joseph with his

---

160   Introduction, The Book of Mormon.

face buried in the hat, dictating from stones like the ones they had used in treasure hunting, with a blanket hung across the room and his daughter Emma taking dictation on the other side. Mr. Hale was livid. While Emma and Joseph's parents, as well as a few close friends, seem to have taken his vision and the golden Bible seriously, Mr. Hale never ceased to regard Joseph as an arrogant fraud.

Two and a half years and 275,000 words later, when Joseph was twenty-four, the translation was completed. The Book of Mormon was finally published in 1830. But Joseph needed witnesses to his claim that the golden plates actually existed. Eventually, three witnesses testified to having seen the golden plates: "an angel of God came down from heaven" and laid the plates with their strange inscriptions before their eyes. One of the three later said he had seen the plates only with the eye of faith while they were covered with a cloth. Joseph got a statement from eight other witnesses who claimed to have "seen and hefted" the golden plates.[161] Three of these eight came from Smith's family and included his father. The rest all came from the Whitmer family, who were close to the Smiths. Joseph's wife, Emma, never signed as a witness. New movements and religions often begin with the close friends and family of the founder who are not strongly attached to an existing religious community.[162] Mormonism was no exception, and Joseph was far from the only person in the Palmyra area who claimed to have visions. None of the eleven witnesses ever retracted their early testimony. In 1838, another witness wrote that none of the witnesses had literally seen the plates with their physical eyes.[163] It is not clear that anyone ever actually saw the plates without some sort of cover over them, and

161   Ibid., 26; Brodie, *No Man Knows My History*, 76–80.
162   Rodney Stark, *The Rise of Christianity* (San Francisco: HarperSanFrancisco, Harper Collins Paperback Ed., 1997), 16–21.
163   Ostling, *Mormon America*, 267.

none ever read or translated what was written on them. Only Joseph, with his magic stones, knew what was written on those plates. Like Muhammed, who claimed that God, through the angel Gabriel, had spoken directly into his ear, Joseph Smith asserted that God spoke directly to him through the stones and he dictated God's word to scribes. That translation, from engravings read only by Joseph, became The Book of Mormon.

The story told by The Book of Mormon is that the Israelite people came to the Americas in two seaborne migrations from the Holy Land: one in around 2200 BC, after the Tower of Babel incident recounted in the Old Testament; the second and later one around 600 BC, just before the Babylonian captivity of the Israelites. After their arrival in the Americas, the Israelites divided into two groups: one, wicked and rebellious, became the Lamenites, whom God cursed with a dark skin and who, according to Moroni, were the ancestors of the American Indians. The second group, the so-called Nephites, remained obedient and faithful. The Book of Mormon describes how the Nephites built a great civilization of cities and temples and roads. The Nephites were often at war with the Lamenites, but Jesus, after his resurrection in Jerusalem, came to America to preach his gospel to the Lamenites and the Nephites and establish his true church in the Western Hemisphere. When the true gospel was delivered, Jesus rose to heaven and a united Christian commonwealth flourished in the Americas for several centuries.

Eventually, sin and apostasy renewed the division between Lamanites and Nephites, a division which culminated in a great battle at the Hill Cumorah, near Palmyra, New York, in the year 400 CE. The Nephites were crushingly defeated. But the last surviving Nephite, a general, and apparently an angel, hid the golden plates, which tell the Nephite story. These were to be revealed to a latter-day prophet some fifteen centuries later. That prophet, needless to say, was a then seventeen-year-old Joseph Smith, Jr. When Joseph had completed his work of "translation," he returned the golden book to the surviving Nephite, the angel Moroni, who then took it up to heaven.

The Book of Mormon came under critical fire almost from the day it was published. There were many Indian burial mounds around Palmyra, and there were endless stories of buried treasure hidden in some of them. It was also widely believed that the American Indians were descendants of the Hebrews. Ethan Smith had written a popular book called *View of the Hebrews*. His theory of the origin of those mounds was almost exactly the same as the story in The Book of Mormon: they contained relics of ancient Hebrew civilization. There are, in fact, remarkable parallels between Joseph Smith's The Book of Mormon and Ethan Smith's *View of the Hebrews*, including a Hebrew migration, which brought a large degree of civilization to the Indians; the tale of Indians who fell back into the barbarous ways of hunting; and the annihilation of most of the more civilized Indians. There was even a story of a book that had been preserved for a long time and buried somewhere with an Indian chief.[164]

Most damning of all is that the golden plates that Joseph claimed to be translating from the "reformed Egyptian" were purported to be a document written in 400 CE, more than one thousand years before Columbus arrived in the Americas. Joseph Smith dictated large sections of the 1769 King James Bible from his golden plates, especially from Isaiah, Matthew, Hebrews, the Beatitudes, and the Sermon on the Mount. Joseph Smith and most Americans of his

---

164   Brodie, *No Man*, 46–47.

era were very familiar with the King James Bible. In The Book of Mormon, even textual errors, which are unique to the 1769 edition of the King James Bible, are reproduced.[165] For loyal Mormons, however, The Book of Mormon is a revelation from God and its story is literally and historically true. It is impossible, they argue, that an uneducated rural teenager could have written that brilliant piece of religious literature. It *had* to have come from God! The Koran suffered from similar attacks: how could an illiterate Arab merchant have written the marvelous rhymed revelations of the Koran?

The difficulty here is that extensive research has yet to uncover any document that predates the 1830 publication of The Book of Mormon that mentions Joseph Smith's first vision of God and Jesus Christ[166] or his second vision when the angel Moroni told him of the golden plates. One author pointed out in 1840 that in the twenty years since Joseph claimed to have had his vision (1820), he had become a highly visible and controversial figure. His supporters defended him, and his enemies defamed him. Joseph preached constantly, offering revelation after revelation from God. But no one in this long period so much as hinted that he had heard the story of Joseph's first vision and the two gods. Despite Joseph's claim that he was vilified and persecuted for telling of his vision, the event seems to have "passed totally unnoticed in Joseph's home town."[167] Joseph, in fact, ignored the vision entirely in several early versions of the church's beginning. Fawn Brodie says that twenty-five years after her book on Joseph Smith came out in 1945, a "dedicated search" in newspapers and manuscripts had uncovered no document that mentions Joseph Smith's first vision of God and Jesus Christ

---

165   Ostling, *Mormon America*, 267–268.
166   Julius Pamphlet, 26.
167   Brodie, *No Man, Supplement*, 405.

written before the publication of The Book of Mormon.[168] If Joseph ever told anyone about his vision, as he claimed, no one mentioned it—at least not in writing.

Critics also argue that Joseph, like most people from Bible-reading families, was familiar with the King James Bible and had probably at least heard of the enormously popular book by Ethan Smith, *View of the Hebrews*. Joseph also shared the popular curiosity about Indians and the possibility that they might be descendants of the lost tribes of Israel. His siblings recalled that as a child, he told fascinating stories about Indians, treasure hunting, and so forth. In short, it is perfectly possible that Joseph Smith could write The Book of Mormon on his own, without God's help.

Since The Book of Mormon purports to be the word of God, we have to face the fact that there is not a shred of evidence for the story told in it. There is no evidence of two great seaborne migrations from the Middle East to the Americas. There is no DNA evidence of any link between Hebrews and American Indians. There is no vestige of either Hebrew or Egyptian in the language of the American Indians. There are no ruins or other archeological evidence from the great cities described in The Book of Mormon. There is no proof that "a single person, place, or event unique to Joseph Smith's 'gold Bible'" has ever existed.[169] Michael D. Coe, a secular scholar familiar with The Book of Mormon concludes: "The bare facts of the matter are that nothing, absolutely nothing, has ever shown up in any New World excavation which would suggest to a dispassionate observer that The Book of Mormon, as claimed by Joseph Smith,

---

168   Ibid., 405–406. Brodie gives a summary of the evidence on this point in a special summary in the 1971 and 1995 editions of her book.
169   Ostling, *Mormon America*, 254–259.

is a historical document relating to the history of early migrants to our hemisphere."[170]

Moreover, The Book of Mormon is full of anachronisms: the wheel described by Joseph was not used for work in pre-Columbian America; the horse did not come until the Spanish conquest; and there is no archeological evidence for plants, such as wheat, that are described in The Book of Mormon or for the metallurgy involving the smelting and casting of the type of steel swords used in The Book of Mormon warfare. The civilization described in The Book of Mormon simply could not have existed in the western hemisphere in 400 CE.

Mormon leaders answer "that the Lord does not intend that the Book of Mormon, at least at the present time, shall be proved true by any archeological findings."[171]

The argument continues to this day. "Were there really gold plates and ministering angels, or was there just Joseph Smith seated at a table with his face in his hat dictating to a scribe a fictional account of the ancient inhabitants of the Americas?"[172] From its beginnings, the church has declared it essential that The Book of Mormon be accepted as it presented itself, as historical fact, not inspired fiction. Loyal Mormons accept this. No excavation has ever produced any evidence for the great battle that was supposed to have taken place at the Hill of Cumorah near Palmyra, New York, in 400 CE, but loyal Mormons "know" that the battle took place there: "The first time you walk on the grounds, you know something

---

170 Quoted at ibid., 273.
171 Quoted at ibid., 273.
172 Ibid., 259.

big happened here.... I believe the battle did take place here. It's just something I feel."[173]

If Jesus came to the New World after his resurrection, where does that leave traditional Christianity? The official Mormon position is that after the death of the last apostle, the Christian movement collapsed into apostasy, led by sinners and charlatans. Western Christianity, in short, cannot be the church of Jesus. Jesus, after his resurrection, came to the New World to build his true church, the Church of Latter-Day Saints, whose doctrine is true doctrine, and that doctrine is distinctly different from that of traditional mainline Christian churches.

The original The Book of Mormon portrays a fairly conventional God and Jesus, except for the collapse of the original Palestinian church and the preaching of the true gospel in the New World. There was a father, son, and holy ghost, and large sections of the King James Bible were incorporated in the original The Book of Mormon. There is no mention of polygamy or multiple gods or baptism of the dead in The Book of Mormon. But the Mormon Church preaches a continuing revelation, and Joseph Smith poured forth a series of further revelations, including the startling revelation that Jackson County, Missouri, was the site of the biblical Garden of Eden.[174]

Perhaps the most shocking revelation is the one on polygamy, or plural wives, as the Mormons prefer to call it. Joseph Smith seems to have taken his first plural wife in 1833, when he was twenty-seven. In 1835, while Joseph was visiting Michigan, the church assembly unanimously passed an anti-polygamy resolution. The practice

---

173 Quoted at ibid., 271.
174 Ostling, *Mormon America*, 30.

nonetheless continued, albeit discretely. Church authorities later came out in the open by adopting a scriptural revelation permitting a plurality of wives. Joseph may have had more than thirty wives; Brigham Young had at least twenty. Church elders thought nothing of choosing other men's wives, their colleagues' daughters, and often, mere teenaged girls. The process, in most cases, was emotionally brutal. It would begin with Joseph or Brigham Young or some other church elder telling the proposed wife that their marriage was a "command of God" and that to refuse would lead to her destruction, or damnation, or as Joseph put it to the seventeen-year-old Lucy Walker, "It is a command of God to you. I will give you until tomorrow to decide this matter. If you reject this message, the gate will be closed forever against you."[175] Finally, in 1890, in order to gain statehood for Utah, the Mormon Church renounced the practice of polygamy but retained the principle as an ideal.[176] Mormon polygamy shows how easy it is in a tight-knit community for powerful church leaders to use "the word of God" to get people to do almost anything in order to remain in the community.

Joseph Smith organized his new church in New York state in May of 1829 and officially formed it on April 6, 1830, in Fayette, New York, with about thirty followers present. Almost immediately, two early elders, Oliver Cowdery and Hiram Page, also claimed to have revelations from God and even demanded that some of Joseph's revelations be amended. Joseph squashed that challenge immediately. He must have been a formidable presence, for he was able to make both men back down by professing to speak the Lord's word: "no one shall be appointed to receive commandments and revelations in this Church, excepting my servant Joseph Smith, Jun, for he received

---

175   Brodie, *No Man*, 337; Ostling, *Mormon America*, 62–63.
176   Brodie, *No Man*, 40.

them even as Moses." Joseph was not challenged again. From that time forward, the only source of authority in the church was Joseph Smith, "first president, prophet, seer, and revelator." After Joseph was murdered when a mob attacked him in jail, his successors in that office, beginning with Brigham Young, assumed sole authority.[177]

In 1835, a traveling showman came through Kirtland displaying four Egyptian mummies and some papyri. Smith bought them and made the papyri the basis of another spiritual translation. He claimed that when he was finished translating the Egyptian writing of the papyri he had purchased, one of them turned out to be the Old Testament book of Abraham. There is, of course, no book of Abraham in the Old Testament (Genesis tells the Abraham story at length), and it was duly incorporated into Mormon scripture.[178]

The newly discovered book of Abraham was published in the late 1850s and was almost immediately exposed as a sham. The facsimiles of the papyri on which the translation was said to be based and some of Smith's more recent revelations taken from *Doctrine and Covenants* were put together in a collection entitled the *Pearl of Great Price*. It quickly appeared that the papyri were ordinary Egyptian funerary documents that had nothing whatever to do with the nonexistent book of Abraham. Virtually all authorities who looked at the papyri agreed that Smith's interpretation had nothing to do with the papyri. His claim that he had uncovered the book of Abraham was simply nonsense. Why, in any case, would the work of an Old Testament Hebrew prophet be translated into Egyptian and buried with an Egyptian mummy?[179] The Ostlings write that facsimiles of the papyri are still published with the *Pearl of Great*

177 Brodie, *No Man*, 92; Ostling, *Mormon America*, 29.
178 Brodie, *No Man*, 184; Ostling, *Mormon America*, 31.
179 Brodie, *No Man*, 280–281.

Price, but the current pamphlet version appears to have dropped them, as well as Joseph Smith's original head note claiming that the papyri were "the writings of Abraham while he was in Egypt ... written by his own hand."[180]

When the "original Old Testament book of Abraham" was shown to be nothing of the kind, one would have thought that there would be a mass exodus from the church, at least among the liberals and intellectuals. There wasn't. "Why?" asks Klaus Hansen, a Mormon professor at Queen's University, Ontario. "Because," he says, "cultural Mormons ... do not believe in the historical authenticity of the Mormon scriptures in the first place. So there is nothing to disconfirm." Hansen cites Frank Kermode's observation "that even the most devastating act of disconfirmation will have no affect whatever on true Believers."[181] Rodney Stark, who has made careful studies of the rise of new movements and religions, argues that "questions of literal historicity are not central to the Mormon religion."[182]

Neither is doctrinal stability. In his most famous sermon, preached just a few weeks before he was murdered in 1844, Joseph Smith made substantial additions to Mormon doctrine. "God himself was once as we are now," he proclaimed, "and is an exalted Man, and sits enthroned in yonder heavens."[183] God is a man of flesh and blood and not some ineffable spirit. He has a body; he has a face; he spoke face-to-face with Abraham. "Our sacred books teach that not only was Jesus Christ in the beginning with God, but that the spirits of all men were also with him in the beginning, and that these

---

180   Ostling, *Mormon America*, 279; Joseph Smith, *Pearl of Great Price* (Filiquarian Publishing, LLC, 2006).
181   Quoted in ibid., 283–284.
182   Quoted in Ostling, *Mormon America*, 263.
183   "King Follet Discourse," quoted in Ostling, 388.

sons of God, as well as the Lord Jesus Christ, became incarnated in bodies of flesh and bone."[184] Men and women had living souls that preexisted their mortality. When they finish their mortal lives and die, they will be wholly restored in every detail, down to the last molecule, and rejoin their departed ancestors. Moreover, any man or woman can, step-by-step, exalt himself or herself to be a god, as God did. The process of exaltation does not end with death; after death, humankind can continue exalting itself until all or most are gods. It follows that there must be many gods in the hereafter. Mormons reject the label "polytheism." What they claim is a plurality of gods. Moreover, Mormons now believe you can baptize the dead so that they can be given the choice of joining the church and exalting themselves after death.

The Book of Mormon having been dictated from "seer stones," the proclamation of revelations from God just when Joseph needed them, and the patent fraud of Joseph's discovery of the book of Abraham led to constant debate over whether Joseph Smith was a prophet or a fraud. It is just possible that he was neither. Given the wild mix of religions, diviners, prophets, occult magicians, and hucksters that Smith grew up with and his fondness for fanciful tales, he may just have told a story about a golden Bible and a lost civilization that, to his amazement, some people believed. He played the role and embellished the story as he had all through his youth and found himself at the head of a small but determined band of believers. He may have come to feel responsible for them; he may even have come to believe his stories of the Nephites and Moroni and the golden Bible. We will never know.[185] Martin Marty, a sympathetic non-Mormon and wide-ranging religious scholar, thinks the whole

---

184   *Doctrine and Covenants*, 93, quoted in Ostling, 298–299.
185   See the comments of a Catholic scholar quoted in Ostling's *Mormon America*, 27, and their own comments at ibid., 260–263.

88

prophet/fraud argument is irrelevant: what is important is to seek to try to understand Smith's message rather than to debate its literal historicity.[186]

But what, exactly, is the message? The textual Mormonism of Smith's 1830 The Book of Mormon? The *Pearl of Great Price*, which has a human Jesus creating the world in the name of God, a God who speaks to Moses face-to-face as his son and explains that his first son, Jesus, will be the future savior? The 1843 revelation that Old Testament polygamy was to be revived? The theology of the 1844 "King Follett Discourse" with a God and Jesus of flesh and blood and multiple gods? The 1890 revelation that polygamy was no longer to be permitted? The 1978 revelation permitting black men to be Mormon priests? The baptism of the dead, and a post-mortal life that offers the possibility of godhood? Or the twenty-first-century Mormonism, which has become an increasingly assimilated version of mainstream Christianity—a Mormonism where Mitt Romney can say publicly that "I cannot imagine anything more awful than polygamy"?[187]

The official position of the Mormon leadership is clear. Joseph Smith was a prophet; he received revelations from God; and The Book of Mormon is God's word and is based on historical truth. Official Mormon history is therefore fluid; it must proceed along the lines of faith. Not everything that is true is necessarily useful. Church President Ezra Taft Benson warned church teachers against the snares of neutrality and objectivity: "We are entrusting you to

---

186 Ibid., 261–262; Rodney Stark in his *The Rise of Christianity* has made a careful sociological and statistical study of the rise of Christianity, using contemporary religious movements, including the Mormons, as models.

187 Quoted in the *Boston Globe* (June 26, 2007) A7, column 6.

represent the Lord and the First Presidency to your students, not the views of the detractors of the Church."[188]

When the then Mormon president, Gordon B. Hinckley, was asked in 1998 whether he believed in the Christ of other Christians, he replied, "No, I don't. The traditional Christ of whom they speak is not the Christ of whom I speak. For the Christ of whom I speak has been revealed in this the Dispensation of the Fullness of Times."[189]

The Ostlings note that: "There is a very real sense in which the church's history is its theology, and that it is not merely the supernatural events surrounding the church's beginnings with the Angel Moroni and the golden plates at Hill Cumorah." It is everything that has happened to the church ever since and that, according to Mormon elders, is sacred history[190]—the history of believers who record countless tales of persecution and forced migrations in their diaries and are encouraged by the church to do so, so that their suffering will be recorded, and the survival and success of their community displayed. The Book of Mormon, the *Pearl of Great Price*, the revelations, and the "King Follett Discourse" *must* be historically true. They reveal God's word as spoken to Joseph Smith, Jr. Why else would they have suffered so and persevered?

A loyal Mormon does not put his membership in the Mormon community at risk over a disagreement on what really happened. In pagan polytheism, all you had to do was be loyal to the god of your community. The community might worship several gods, just to be safe. It was the god or gods of your community that you stayed with, because it was your community that helped you live

---

188   Quoted in Ostling, *Mormon America*, 249.
189   Prothero, 197.
190   Ostling, *Mormon America*, 245.

your life. Given the multiplicity of religions, churches, and religious positions the modern world has to choose from, it seems to me that that is still true. Church members can ignore the historicity of the founding myths, and they often do, but they cannot walk away from the community and its traditions and rituals. A recent book argues that religion is an evolutionary development that makes human communities more cohesive and comforting and safe.[191] If that argument is valid, then whether God exists and the historicity of sacred scripture is largely irrelevant. What matters is that you find safety and comfort in your community of believers.

191 Wade, *The Faith Instinct.*

SIX

SCIENCE'S CREATION STORY

"Once upon a time, some 13–20 billion years ago, our Universe began in what has become known as the 'Hot Big Bang,'"[192] when, in an infinitesimal fraction of a second, what eventually became the entire universe erupted from a subatomic particle so tiny it would make a grain of sand look colossal.[193] That story almost makes Genesis look good, but its general outline is now widely accepted by the scientific community, and although there are gaps, critical portions of that story have been confirmed by observation and laboratory experiments.

NASA recently reported sending a robotic probe into space that detected light created in the early universe, which has been traveling for more than thirteen billion years—the aftereffects of the energy event scientists say gave birth to the universes some 13.7 billion

---

192   Walter H. Waller and Paul W. Hodge, *Galaxies and the Cosmic Frontier* (Cambridge, MA: Harvard University Press, 2003), 239.
193   Brian Greene, *The Elegant Universe* (New York: Vintage Press, 1999), 4.

years ago. That early universe was an astonishingly empty sea of nothingness: no planets, no stars, no galaxies, and only infinitesimal variations in temperature. "We have new evidence that the universe suddenly grew from submicroscopic to astronomical size in less than the blink of an eye," said the lead investigator. "This tremendous inflation of the universe happened in much less than a trillionth of a second."[194] What the NASA probe detected were the earliest traces of science's creation story.

Science's creation story does not require us to choose between the voice of God and the ancient tales of humankind. It starts with a number of observable facts, which, so far, no one seriously doubts. First, the universe is expanding. If you could run time backward, you would eventually contract the universe down to the immensely hot, dense energy event from which the observable universe suddenly emerged. Second, the universe is immense, so immense that astronomers measure its distances in light years, which is the distance light can travel in one year—some 5,888 trillion miles. Our galaxy, which is only one of billions of galaxies, is 100,000 light years across: 100,000 times 5,888 trillion miles, an almost unimaginable distance. It takes light from a star on one side of our galaxy a hundred thousand years to reach an observer on the other side. A neighboring galaxy, the Andromeda, is about two million light years away. The light we can see from that galaxy started out two million years ago! Astronomers, by looking out into space, look back in time.

The real mystery lies in that first instant of creation. "[I]f we leave aside, for the moment, the puzzle of exactly what happened in the first split second of creation itself, our observations of the

---

194   As reported in the *Boston Globe*, Friday, March 15, 2006, A10.

expanding Universe are entirely adequate to tell us that the creation must have occurred between 10 and 20 billion years ago";[195] after that, "cosmology provides an elegant, consistent, and calculationally tractable framework for understanding the universe as far back as the briefest moments after the bang."[196]

But what would cause such an extraordinary event? Not God, apparently, but a quantum vacuum fluctuation. According to quantum theory, "At the smallest scales, subatomic particles sometimes emerge instantaneously" and then disappear. Quantum physics, we are told, can analyze these odd jumps into and out of existence with great precision, "but it cannot explain them in ways that make sense at the human level."[197] That is what theologians say about God! But the scientists have a methodology: their theories on the physical laws of the universe have been tested in the laboratory; the behavior of subatomic particles can be tested in particle accelerators; and their theories can be expressed in mathematical equations, which have demonstrated enormous predictive power.

At one time, theologians could have objected that the scientific method was limited to the material, measurable, physical world, but that objection may no longer hold. Albert Einstein was shocked to learn, in the 1940s, that his famous equation, $E=mc^2$ meant that energy and matter are equivalent, and that, therefore, a star could be created out of nothing since the energy of its mass is exactly balanced by the energy of its gravitational field.[198] When the immensity of

---

195   John Gribbin, *In Search of the Big Bang*, New Ed. (New York and London: Penguin Press, 1998), 170.

196   Ibid., 352–353.

197   David Christian, *Maps of Time: An Introduction to Big History* (Berkeley, CA: University of California Press, 2004, 2005), 17.

198   *Christopher Potter, You Are Here: A Portable History of the Universe* (Harper: 2009), 151.

the universe and the invisibly tiny world of quantum mechanics are combined, they can be explained only in mathematical formulae that almost no one understands: "Our modern-day materialist creation story has become so abstruse that it may need a poet to do it justice." Mystics have been arguing that for centuries. Today, mathematics is the language of science, and it is increasingly untranslatable even among large groups of scientists.[199]

I have made this small digression simply to point out that the language and rules of engagement in science are far more civilized than they are in religious disputes. To challenge religious authority can mean exile or death; in science, you can win a Nobel Prize for successfully challenging the accepted wisdom.

The idea that the universe was the result of a quantum vacuum fluctuation that did not stop was first proposed by a young physicist named Edward B. Tryan in the late 1960s. His suggestion was ignored for several years, but cosmologists gradually began working on it because, among other reasons, there was no better explanation for an expanding universe and because quantum theory posits a vacuum that is not really a vacuum but a frothing sea of unpredictably volatile energy, which periodically erupts into particles and antiparticles, which almost instantly annihilate one another, which creates more energy to create more particles, which again annihilate one another, again releasing energy, and so on and so on. Intriguing as it was, there were a number of problems with the idea of the universe arising from a vacuum fluctuation. For one thing, vacuum fluctuations were subatomic in size and the universe is huge. Given the estimated age of the universe and its estimated rate of expansion at the time Tryan made his suggestion, the original big bang theory did not get you to

---

199   Ibid., 159.

a universe that was as big as the one that could be observed—and even what we can observe is but a small part of the whole.

During the 1980s, Alan H. Guth, who was not trained in cosmology but in particle physics and quantum theory, was working on the problem of the creation of matter. It occurred to Guth that almost all the problems with the big bang theory could be solved if you assumed that in the initial expansion, there was a trillionth of a trillionth of a second in which space expanded at a rate greater than the speed of light to a size greater than the presently observable universe. Once that period of inflation was over, Guth's inflationary theory, as it became known, merged smoothly with the big bang theory, "which for several decades has been the generally accepted picture of cosmic evolution."[200]

His inflationary theory, Guth argues, shows how the entire universe could evolve from an initial seed weighing about an ounce and having a diameter more than a billion times smaller than a proton. While Guth is understandably enthusiastic about his inflationary theory, note that he is not proposing sacred doctrine or a new religion but merely what seems to be a useful hypothesis, which will have to be tested by further observation and analysis:

> While the final verdict on inflationary cosmology is not yet in, the basic outline of the theory seems very persuasive. The theory not only accounts for the vast amount of matter in the universe but offers plausible explanations for a number of features of the universe. If inflation theory is correct, then the inflationary mechanism is responsible for the creation

---

200 Alan H. Guth, *The Inflationary Universe* (Reading, MA: Helix Books, 1997), 14.

of essentially all the matter and energy in the universe. The theory also implies that the observed universe is only a minute fraction of the entire universe.

The universe is so immense and is expanding at such speed that we can see only those events from which the light has had time to reach us.[201] Moreover, the "universe could have evolved from absolutely nothing consistent with all known conservation laws. While no detailed scientific creation theory is known, the possibility of developing such a theory now appears open."[202] You almost never see a religious argument put as tentatively as that.

Most cosmologists are now persuaded that the universe began the way Alan Guth's inflationary hypothesis says it began, but they would be open to an alternative explanation if it were equally plausible—and testable—and explained more of what was going on in the physical universe.

Guth asks, "How far back should we trust the equations of the big bang theory?"[203] Others worry that "the more we look at the evidence, the more we are compelled to imagine both space and time emerging from some sort of hyper-space-time—what cosmologists today term the quantum vacuum. Otherwise, we are left pondering religious issues."[204] What they mean by "religious issues," of course, are the kinds of creation stories that can be neither tested nor observed. For a scientist, that is the equivalent of saying, "I don't know what happened." That is also true for theologians.

---

201 Guth, *The Inflationary Universe*, 15; Ferris, *Coming of Age in the Milky Way*, note at 360.
202 Guth, *The Inflationary Universe*, 12.
203 Ibid., 88.
204 Waller and Hodge, *Galaxies and the Cosmic Frontier*, 244.

"That anything exists at all is the primordial mystery that points to God."[205] And God, of course, is utterly unknowable.

But the big bang really happened. Using the big bang equations, cosmologists have extrapolated all the way back to one second after the big bang and estimated its temperature at over 10 billion degrees. After the end of the first seven days, the universe was at 17 million degrees, a million degrees hotter than the center of the sun. Even one hundred thousand years after the big bang, the universe was about the same temperature as the surface of the sun: 5,800 degrees Kelvin.[206] Scientists long puzzled over why the helium abundance throughout the entire universe was never more or less than about 23 percent of all matter. Hydrogen fusion is a well-known physical process and has been tested in the laboratory. It has been calculated that it takes very high pressures and temperatures of 10 billion degrees or more to make helium from hydrogen. As the universe cooled and expanded and density and pressure dropped, helium production would have ceased. The intense conditions of the hot big bang only lasted long enough to create a helium abundance of 23 percent. If everything in the universe came from the hot big bang, nothing in the universe should have a helium abundance of less than 23 percent. The helium abundance of even the oldest objects in the universe is now firmly fixed at 23 to 24 percent. All matter in the universe, therefore, came out of the hot big bang.[207]

In October 1996, Pope John Paul II announced that scientific research had led to the "recognition of the theory of evolution as

---

205 Johnson, *The Creed*, 96.
206 Guth, *The Inflationary Universe*, 86.
207 Martin Rees, *Before the Beginning* (Reading, MA: Helix Books, 1997), 56–57.

more than just a hypothesis."[208] If evolution is going to be recognized by Roman Catholic doctrine or any other Bible-based religion, then there is no historical Adam, no historical Eve, no Garden of Eden, and no fall from grace to bring on original sin. If there is no original sin, there is no reason for God to bring down his son to help restore humankind. Roman Catholicism and Christianity have not yet come that far, but it is clear they are on the cusp of a major theological revolution. The entire biblical story of creation will have to be abandoned. "Once one has grasped the nature of Scripture, and let go of the idea that all its stories are literally true, the biggest problem for Christians is removed."[209] But the mystery of the universe that exists still hauntingly remains.

Having gotten our many religious creation myths out of the way, I would like to close by quoting another scientist. They seem to have become our modern theologians. Steven Weinberg, flying over the country, reflected that: "It is very hard to realize that this is all just a tiny part of an overwhelmingly hostile universe. It is even harder to realize that this present universe has evolved from an unspeakably unfamiliar early condition, and faces a future extinction of endless cold or intolerable heat. The more the universe seems comprehensible, the more it also seems pointless."[210]

We shall have to live with that. There is nothing out there.

---

208   Jerry D. Korsmeyer, *Evolution and Eden* (New York: Paulist Press, 1998), 20.
209   Ibid., 72.
210   Steven Weinberg, *The First Three Minutes* (New York: Basic Books, 1993), 154.